8/03

D0880973

An Imagist at War

An Imagist at War

The Complete War Poems
of Richard Aldington

Selected
with an Introduction and Notes
by Michael Copp

Madison • Teaneck
Fairleigh Dickinson University Press
London: Associated University Presses

Associated University Presses
440 Forsgate Drive
Cranbury, NJ 08512

Associated University Presses
16 Barter Street
London WC1A 2AH, England

Associated University Presses
P.O. Box 338, Port Credit
Mississauga, Ontario
Canada L5G 4L8

The paper used in this publication meets the requirements of the American National Standard for Permanence of Paper for Printed Library Materials Z39.48-1984.

Library of Congress Cataloging-in-Publication Data

Aldington, Richard, 1892–1962.
    An imagist at war : the complete war poems of Richard Aldington / selected with an introduction and notes by Michael Copp.
        p.   cm.
    Includes bibliographical references (p.) and index.
    ISBN 0-8386-3952-6 (alk. paper)
    1. World War, 1914–1918—Poetry.   2. War poetry, English.   I. Copp, Michael.   II. Title.
PR6001.L4 A6   2002
821'.912—dc21   2002024035

PRINTED IN THE UNITED STATES OF AMERICA

For Alan and John,
In Friendship

Contents

Part II: Additional Poems

Part III: Prose Poems

Part IV: Fragments from Longer Poems

Acknowledgments

I AM INDEBTED TO THE FOLLOWING FOR PERMISSION TO INCLUDE copyright material:

Catherine Aldington, for permission to include poems by Richard Aldington.

Norman T. Gates, for permission to include material from his *Richard Aldington: An Autobiography in Letters,* and *The Poetry of Richard Aldington: A Critical Evaluation and an Anthology of Uncollected Poems.*

Caroline Zilboorg, for permission to include material from her *Richard Aldington & H.D.: The Early Years in Letters,* and *Richard Aldington & H.D.: The Later Years in Letters.*

Every effort has been made to obtain permission from copyright holders before publication. Any inadvertent omissions or errors will be rectified at the earliest opportunity.

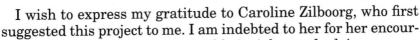

I wish to express my gratitude to Caroline Zilboorg, who first suggested this project to me. I am indebted to her for her encouragement as well as for her valuable insights and advice.

An Imagist at War

Introduction

Bᴇꜰᴏʀᴇ ᴀᴘᴘʀᴏᴀᴄʜɪɴɢ Aʟᴅɪɴɢᴛᴏɴ's ᴡᴀʀ ᴘᴏᴇᴛʀʏ ɪᴛ ᴡɪʟʟ ʙᴇ ᴜsᴇꜰᴜʟ to consider his later prose writings about the war. His novel, *Death of a Hero*, 1929, and his collection of short stories, *Roads to Glory*, 1930, were written and published some time after his war poetry and at the height of the outpouring of novels and memoirs dealing with the war. Aldington saw a thread running through much of his war writing, and he was anxious for others to be aware of this linkage between his poetry and his prose. On 16 March 1933 he wrote to Eric Warman: "You will see how the War Poems [1919] and Fool i' the Forest [1924] lead up to Death of a Hero [1929]."[1]

The brief analyses of *Death of a Hero* and *Roads to Glory* are followed by an outline of Aldington's war service and of his reaction to this experience as expressed in letters to his first wife and friends, and in his autobiography. The introductory survey of his war poetry covers (a) the writing and publication of the war poems; (b) his emotional and professional relationship with the expatriate American poet, H.D. (Hilda Doolittle), to whom he was married; and (c) the role he played in the inception, development, and practice of Imagism. The ninety-six poems are divided into five sections: Early Poems (7), *Images of War* (44), Additional Poems (24), Prose Poems (17), and Fragments from Longer Poems (4). A short introduction to each of these sections focuses on selected poems that embody the key elements and qualities of Aldington's war poetry.

Wᴀʀ Lɪᴛᴇʀᴀᴛᴜʀᴇ: Tʜᴇ Bᴏᴏᴍ Yᴇᴀʀs

Richard Aldington is probably best remembered as the author of *Death of a Hero*. Published in September 1929, this novel—his first—is generally regarded as one of the best of the fictional treatments of the Great War. It lifted him immediately into the category of best-selling novelist (three months later, in December 1929, sales had passed the ten thousand figure). This book confirmed his international reputation, and one indeed that stretched beyond the confines of the English-speaking world, since by 1932 the novel had been translated into German, Swedish, French, and Russian.[2] It continued to be read widely decades later. On 20 October 1961, Aldington wrote to his brother Tony: "Hero is still in print in English, Russian, Czech, Italian. There are translations in 14 different languages."[3]

~

The flood of prose writing about the war—fiction and memoirs especially, but also journals and diaries—belongs for the most part to the years 1926–33, that is, approximately a decade after the Armistice. The bulk of the war poetry (including most of Aldington's) had already been written and published considerably earlier, towards the end of the war and in the early 1920s. An even narrower span of time, the years 1928–30 in particular, saw the publication of a number of prose works, many of which are now universally accepted as classics of war literature:

1928
Edmund Blunden, *Undertones of War*
Ford Madox Ford, *Last Post* (the final volume in the four-part *Parade's End*)
Arnold Zweig, *The Case of Sergeant Grischa* (translated from the German, *Der Streit um den Sergeanten Grischa*, 1928)

1929
Richard Aldington, *Death of a Hero*
Mary Borden, *The Forbidden Zone*
Rudolf Binding, *A Fatalist at War* (translated from the German, *Aus dem Kriege*)
Charles Edmonds (C. E. Carrington), *A Subaltern's War*
Robert Graves, *Goodbye to All That*
Ernest Hemingway, *A Farewell to Arms*
Ernst Jünger, *Storm of Steel* (translated from the German, *In Stahlgewittern*, 1920)
Frederic Manning, *The Middle Parts of Fortune* (a limited, unexpurgated edition)

16

Erich Maria Remarque, *All Quiet on the Western Front* (translated from the German, *Im Westen Nichts Neues*, 1929)
Ludwig Renn, *War* (translated from the German, *Krieg*, 1928)
R. C. Sherriff, *Journey's End*

1930

Richard Aldington, *Roads to Glory*
Edmund Blunden, *De Bello Germanico*
Frederic Manning, *Her Privates We* (a bowdlerized version of *The Middle Parts of Fortune*)
Siegfried Sassoon, *Memoirs of an Infantry Officer*
Helen Zenna Smith, *Not So Quiet . . . Stepdaughters of War*
H. M. Tomlinson, *All Our Yesterdays*
Henry Williamson, *A Patriot's Progress*

Aldington was alert to the commercial possibilities of *Death of a Hero.* In May 1929 he sent a telegram to his American agent mentioning the great success of R. C. Sherriff's *Journey's End.* Aldington thought that a major English war novel if published in the present climate, would be equally successful. He was anxious for *Death of a Hero* to be brought out as soon as possible, so as to take advantage of the favorable circumstances.[4]

What are the reasons for this great outpouring at this particular time? By way of attempting to answer this question, Samuel Hynes makes a number of suggestions. Firstly, in a general sense, the past needs a lapse of time to become history; thus the narratives of the war required a ten-year gestation period. Secondly, the specific horrors of war demanded a lengthy distancing in time before they could be tackled and shaped. Thirdly, the flood of writing can be seen as the delayed attempt to exorcise the past. Fourthly, the sense of anticipation of a possible future war gave an urgency and purpose to telling the story of the war.[5]

Modris Eksteins goes further. He argues that this great outpouring was occasioned by a mixture of "aspiration, anxiety and doubt." He also stresses that the best war books were written from the individual, rather than national, point of view. This was the only level on which the war could have any meaning. It was the literature of the imagination, not the historical record, which produced the significant works that reconsidered the meaning of the war.[6]

Aldington comments on the reason for this ten-year gap in a

letter, addressed to the dramatist Halcott Glover, that serves as the foreword to *Death of a Hero*. He recalls how he embarked on the book in Belgium just after the Armistice. However, the problems Aldington experienced in readjusting to civilian life caused him to abandon it. It was ten years later that the impulse returned to begin his book again. (7)

In his autobiography Aldington explains in more detail the urge to take up the theme of war once more, this time in a novel. He was living at Port Crau, feeling contented and full of energy. He now felt ready to expand the scale of the aspects of the war that he had put into his poems. Aldington saw himself as playing but a tiny supporting role in a vast tragedy. Now he could grasp how necessary the lapse of time had been for him to be able to assimilate and order his experiences. He indicated that he would employ free expression and satire, and that his novel would be constructed along the lines of the movements of a symphony. He also pointed out that by revealing the tragic outcome at the beginning he would be following the principles of Greek tragedy construction. (331–32) Aldington also underlines the therapeutic effect of writing *Death of a Hero*. It enabled him to purge his system of dangerous material that he felt had been poisoning him for a decade. Having completed the novel, and having, in places, let off a considerable amount of steam, he felt the relief, easing of pressure, and serenity that follows a thunderstorm. (339)

DEATH OF A HERO

In places a pessimistic, angry, cynical, and disillusioned book, it is written in a strongly satirical mode. The war and its aftermath remained with Aldington for a long time. Six years after the publication of *Death of a Hero*, on 11 May 1935, Aldington wrote to his editor and friend A. S. Frere to tell him how surprised he had been to discover to what extent bitterness and resentment concerning long-past events were still gnawing away at him. But he insisted that life's defeats have to be transformed into victories, the prime example in his life being his war experience. For many years he felt that the war had destroyed him as a creative artist, but in the end it provided him with his revenge in the form of his war novel, *Death of a Hero*.[7]

In the Prologue and in Parts I and II, Aldington attacks Victorian and Edwardian establishment attitudes, thought, and behavior, for example their hypocrisy, ignorance, narrowness, and philistinism, or as the narrator puts it, "the Kiplingesque or kicked-backside-of-the-Empire principle." (227) In addition he frequently inserts authorial passages of a condemnatory or sermonizing nature. Aldington's assault on Cant in Part II is a characteristic example of his argumentative, hectoring mode. According to Aldington it was the hypocrisy and duplicity of nineteenth-century society and politics that triggered the war. In this way "Cant, Delusion, and Delirium" proliferated and prevailed for four years. For example, propagandist lies were spread regarding Germany in order to persuade men to fight. (253–54)

Aldington was himself a product of establishment England, having been educated at Dover College, where he would have been subjected to and inculcated with the usual trappings of a public school education, which can be summed up as the OTC (Officers' Training Corps) plus the three C's: Cricket, the Classics, and Christianity. Aldington's knowledge and love of classical myth and literature was to feature strongly in much of his verse, even in some of his war poems. The other two elements, team games and daily acts of worship, would have stressed "manliness," esprit de corps, and unquestioning acceptance of tradition and authority.[8] His distaste for the sort of public school education he received is conveyed in a letter to Amy Lowell on 20 [?] November 1917. His years at Dover College proved to be a very unhappy experience. He found the discipline irksome, his fellow-pupils "futile," and the teaching unimaginative. However, he did admit to enjoying playing rugby, which he ironically described as being the only redeeming feature and purposeful part of the English public school system.[9]

At his minor public school Aldington would have witnessed the development of the future officer class, the young subalterns who would shortly be required to lead their men out of the trenches of the Western Front. One such near contemporary at Dover was Captain Wilfred P. Nevill of the 8th Battalion of the East Surrey Regiment.[10] Aldington regarded such young men, former prefects, house captains and school captains, now subalterns, with a mixture of amused contempt and reluctant admiration, as a passage from *Death of a Hero* reveals. The "hero" Winterbourne has been temporarily assigned a "cushy" job acting as runner for Evans, a young ex-public school officer. This latter figure is portrayed as a typical product of the English public school system, incredibly ignorant, and inhibited, but decent and amiable. Evans had been taught to see where his duty lay and to carry it out, accepting without question the narrow-minded taboos and preconceived ideas of the English middle classes, for example, contempt for all foreigners. In spite of all this Winterbourne cannot help liking Evans, since he possesses a number of positive qualities: he is honest, kindly, conscientious, caring, and inspirational to the men under him. "He could be implicitly relied upon to lead a hopeless attack and to maintain a desperate defence to the very end. There were thousands and tens of thousands like him." (329–31)

Picking up on Aldington's own description of *Death of a Hero* as a "jazz novel," Claire Tylee provides a fair, balanced and perceptive judgment when she says that it "improvises its own form, a combination of narrative and violent political polemic. It has an individual lead voice which is passionate, vehement, strident. Modulating between lyricism and rancour, this is an instrument which refuses to play 'The Last Post' but hectors the reader in a way which critics dislike . . ."[11]

One such group of critics consists of certain feminists who have misread the book as biography and have therefore seen it as containing a criticism of H.D. Another, much wider group, has, from the 1950s onwards, responded negatively to Aldington's work in general. This hostility can be traced back to the publication of Aldington's controversial biography, *Lawrence of Arabia: A Biographical Enquiry*, 1955.

The form of this modernist text has upset some critics and they have subjected the novel to severe censure. In his letter to Halcott Glover that precedes the prologue Aldington anticipates the misunderstandings that the novel's structure will provoke. Self-deprecatingly, he states that his novel has not been written by a professional novelist, that perhaps it is not in fact a novel at all, since it contravenes the conventional form and method of novel writing. He is quite unrepentant about the fact that he has disregarded these conventions. (ix)

George Parfitt finds passages such as the "Cant" extract referred to above dangerously self-indulgent.[12] His negative response appears to be directed both at the author and at his work. Bernard Bergonzi is also hostile, asserting that the novel "lacks coherence and focus," that it fails to marshal the disparate elements (the disillusionment, the iconoclasm, and the debunking tirades) into an orderly whole.[13] One might be forgiven for wondering whether "coherence" is a possible response to the chaos and disjunction of the war. On the other hand, there are many fellow writers who have written approvingly of *Death of a Hero* with its combination of trench realism and passionate denunciations.[14] There are no valid grounds, in fact, for rejecting the binary nature of the novel: "its plot and under-plot, its mixture of exalted, imaginative tragedy and furious misanthropical pamphleteering [. . .] its first part [. . .] filled with passionate indignation against the culpable indifference and selfishness of the pre-war generation, [. . .] its second part [. . .] not less saturated with pity for the helpless victims of their elders' guilt."[15]

Part III concentrates on the front-line experience of the "hero," George Winterbourne, and is written for the most part in a flatter, more restrained mode, producing a more strictly controlled, even documentary narrative. It is indeed the most successful and impressive part of the novel, "the best of Aldington's prose . . . as war literature it deserves the epithet 'great'."[16]

Apart from descriptions of battle and of the destruction of the landscape a great deal of war prose and poetry tackles the subject of male bonding, the close ties between an officer and the men for whom he was responsible, or the friendships that developed between young subalterns. Aldington too treats this theme in *Death of a Hero*. The narrator presents the protagonist, George Winterbourne, as a man who, while detesting everything the war represents, nevertheless finds some compensation in the comradeship of the trenches. One passage, in particular, using much near repetition to emphasize this important point, underlines the fact that in spite of the appalling life the soldiers lived, they had managed to retain their "essential humanity and manhood . . . their essential integrity as men, their essential brotherhood as men." (295–96)

Male bonding and close comradeship inevitably led, in some instances, to homoerotic "crushes." Poets such as Wilfred Owen and Siegfried Sassoon expressed similar stigmatized responses in some of their war poems, albeit in a carefully coded way. Aldington, resolutely and exclusively heterosexual in private life, was anxious to dispel any thoughts of homosexual practices in the close relationships that developed between men at the front.

He unequivocally asserts the platonic purity of such friendships in the "Prologue" to *Death of a Hero*. Aldington saw the relationships that the war effected between men as "real and beautiful and unique." He insists that he "never saw any sign of sodomy," nor did he ever receive any secondhand accounts of such sexual activity. These exceptionally close, undemonstrative examples of comradeship, however, did not carry over into peacetime. (26–27)

Winterbourne is certainly attracted by the sight and proximity of his fellow soldiers whom he describes admiringly, while differentiating them from other male types, the "boudoir rabbits and lounge lizards." (290) He sees his fellow soldiers as "intensely masculine . . . very pure and immensely friendly and stimulating. They had been where no woman and no half-man had ever been, could endure to be . . . They were Men." (290). Trudi Tate regards Aldington's attitude towards homosexual relationships, as exemplified in the above passages, as "hysterical repudiation." This exaggeration seems a distortion, however. She gets closer to what bothers Aldington when she proposes "that homosexuality might be something of a problem for this text."[17] Martin Taylor develops this point in his assessment of Aldington's position vis-à-vis homosexuality. He suggests that Aldington's 1929 reaction is representative of many men of Aldington's generation who found close male bonding when termed homosexual rather than platonic, as uncomfortable and offensive. Taylor unfairly accuses Aldington of lacking in honesty and proper understanding of these emotionally tender relationships, and of being evasive in his treatment of such matters. Such a reading misrepresents Aldington's stance as given in the novel.[18]

Another awkward topic that keeps surfacing in criticism of Aldington's writing, and one that needs to be confronted and refuted, is the accusation of misogyny. A number of war writers were critical of the war attitudes of a certain type of woman, e.g. Siegfried Sassoon ("Glory of Women"), Robert Graves (the "A Little Mother" section in *Goodbye to All That*) and Wilfred Owen ("Disabled" and "S. I. W."). Such an attitude was not confined to male writers. In her poem "Nostra Culpa," written in 1916, Margaret Sackville makes a remarkable assault on her own sex, accusing them of being mainly responsible for the waging of wars: "We spoke not, so men died. / . . . We mothers and we murderers of mankind."[19]

The narrator in *Death of a Hero* condemns women in general as well as, more specifically, Winterbourne's mother, his wife, Elizabeth, and his mistress, Fanny, for what he sees as their hypocrisy, fickleness, unreliability, scheming dishonesty, emotional blackmail, lack of intellectual consistency, and faithlessness. Some commentators have been shocked and offended by what they see as Aldington's unrelenting bitterness towards women in general, expressed in his peculiar contempt for the way women behaved in wartime.[20] From the very start of the novel Winterbourne's mother and women in general receive short shrift. Winterbourne's death, it appears, had an erotic effect on his mother, a reaction attributed to many women in wartime. They responded to the idea of blood, wounds, mud and, suffering in an overwrought manner which frequently expressed itself in "an almost unbearable pitch of amorousness." (12) In *Victoria Station* Winterbourne spots young women embracing soldiers "in a close embrace which at least at that moment was sincere." (396) At the beginning of the novel Elizabeth and Fanny are made to stand as generalized types of womanhood. They are characterized as having adapted to the war with remarkable ease and rapidity, and as possessing "that rather hard efficiency of the war and post-war female," which conceals their "predatory and possessive instincts under a skilful smoke-barrage of Freudian and Havelock Ellis theories." (18–19)

McGreevy has pointed out that whereas most war fiction deals exclusively with the actuality of the soldier's front-line experience, Aldington, in *Death of a Hero*, widens the scene by displaying himself as a fighting man who could treat not only the real physical conditions of the war, but also the social changes brought about in England.[21] One such change is the new-found freedom that a particular class of young women was able to use, or misuse, from the point of view of the narrator of the novel. We should not, however, fall into the trap of extrapolating from Aldington's treatment of the behavior of certain women of a specific class in his writing about the war, and of jumping to the conclusion that they accurately represent his views about, and relationships with, women in his private life or in his other work. The character of Elizabeth as depicted in *Death of a Hero* should not be taken as a portrait of H.D.: "Aldington's abiding affection and deep respect for H.D. as well as his old-fashioned gentlemanly code of discretion when it came to his own sexual relationships prevented his ever treating her satirically."[22]

When we consider how Aldington tackles the depiction of the landscape of war and how he manages to convey to his readers something of the experience of war there are many fine passages to choose from in *Death of a Hero*. In such passages he manages to describe, interpret, and successfully communicate the overwhelming physicality of trench conditions, when all the senses are being assaulted by supra-normal phenomena. At one point, when Winterbourne finds himself in the middle of the devastating onslaught of a preliminary artillery bombardment, Aldington has recourse to the language of music as he seeks to convey the prodigious din of multiple explosions: "a stupendous symphony of sound. . . an immense rhythmic harmony, a super-jazz of tremendous drums, a ride of the Walkyrie played by three thousand cannons. . . the machine-guns played a minor motif of terror. . . colossal harmony." (373)

ROADS TO GLORY

Aldington's thirteen short stories in *Roads to Glory* are less well known than his novel. They were written while he was living in a small hamlet near Toulon and published together in 1930, following the success of *Death of a Hero*. In his autobiography Aldington informs us that he spent the summer "swimming a great deal, walking in the scented *maquis*, translating the *Alcestis* and writing short stories on war themes—a kind of hangover from *Death of a Hero*." (311) This neglected work shows that Aldington, with his novel behind him, had not exhausted what he had to say about the war. He also used the short story form to experiment with various narrative techniques, and in one of them, as instanced below, he dared to intersperse his narrative of the raw facts of war experience with prose poems that use heightened language. David Wilkinson draws attention to the range of style and mood of these stories in which comedy and tragedy alternate, and points to the "grim Kiplingesque humor of 'Killed in Action' " and the "Gissing-like determinism of 'Deserter'."[23]

The title, *Roads to Glory*, echoes a line that comes near the start of Part III of *Death of a Hero*. Winterbourne, at this stage

24

still a private, is sitting in a train with the rest of his draft on their way from Waterloo Station to Folkestone. He passes the time remembering with sardonic amusement various incidents in the early days of training. In one a typically foul-mouthed bayonet instructor berates the inept efforts of a clumsy recruit to dispatch the straw dummy in the approved bloodthirsty manner. The hapless soldier is told to point his bayonet " 'At 'is stummick an' goolies!' " He is also urged to "get down like a fuckin' soldier, and not like a bloody great pross wot's being blocked." At this Winterbourne muses with a smile that "The road to glory was undoubtedly devious in our fair island story." (240)[24]

In the story "The Case of Lieutenant Hall" a fellow officer suggests a visit to sample the delights of the red-light district in Lille. Hall reacts angrily, saying that the sight of so many bodies mangled by war had put him off the sight of any more human flesh. He says that he "hated the thought of women" and that he didn't want any "bloody whores." In his rage he asks rhetorically, "Didn't they urge us into that hell, and do their best to keep us there?" (242)

Hall goes on to specify the target of his hatred—the imperialist cant and jingoist attitudes of the civilians back home. We should recall the women who distributed white feathers to men who had not yet enlisted. Another example is the poster by E. V. Kealey, "Women of Britain Say *GO*," in which a clearly middle-class trio of mother, young wife, and child stare out of a window at a group of soldiers marching off to war. It appears that the attitude expressed by such actions and in such propaganda posters has triggered his rage: "God, how I hate the women, especially those who 'gave' so willingly!" (245)

The concluding story in *Roads to Glory*, "Farewell to Memories," alternates war episodes with poetic prose that seeks to convey the thoughts of one particular soldier, Brandon. In the story the lineation of these passages is as prose, whereas when printed separately they appear as poems (see "Prose Poems," p. 139). The device of using two different voices to contrast the banalities of army routine with the inviolable inner world of the mind and spirit was to be employed later by Henry Reed in his celebrated Second World War poem, "Naming of Parts." In Aldington's story the hard physical toil induces a mood of reverie.[25] Brandon and another soldier, Holme, are detailed to unload bales of hay from a train onto barges. They are uncomfortably hot, the work is back-breaking and dirty, but they are aware of the fragrance wafting from the tightly compressed bales of hay. This is followed by a section of poetic prose that expresses Brandon's nostalgic yearning for the English countryside. He recalls how *"Last June those heavy dried bales waved and glittered in the fields of England."* After enumerating all the wild plants that are crushed in these bales this section ends: *"Dear crushed flowers, dear gentle, perished sisters, speak, whisper, and move, tell me you will dance and whisper for us in the wind next June."* (261–62) Tellingly, Aldington personifies the wild flowers as "sisters." On his return to England he hopes to find flowers and young women as equally consolatory.

Parts of these prose poems first appeared under the title "Prayers and Fantasies I–VIII" in Chicago in November 1918 in *Poetry: A Magazine of Verse* (Vol. 13, No. 2), edited by Harriet Monroe.[26] Most of these prose poems were later included in the volume *The Love of Myrrhine and Konallis, and Other Prose Poems* in 1926. Those that were inserted into the story "Farewell to Memories" in *Roads to Glory* have been brought together under the section "Prose Poems" in the present volume.

PUBLISHING THE WAR POEMS

Even more unfamiliar than this collection of short stories with their passages of prose-poetry are Aldington's war poems, notwithstanding the fact that one recent anthology of war poetry has sought to remedy this neglect and ignorance by generously including fourteen examples.[27] In fact, most of Aldington's considerable literary output has been out of print in recent years: novels, poetry, an autobiography, biographies and short stories as well as critical essays and translations. Various reasons can be adduced for this neglect. First, he wrote no poetry during the last twenty-five years of his life. Second, he chose to live abroad after 1928. Third, and possibly most importantly, in his controversial biography of T. E Lawrence, *Lawrence of Arabia: A Biographical Enquiry*, Aldington presented Lawrence as an "impudent mythomaniac."[28]

At this point it is worthwhile pausing to examine the effect this critical affair had on Aldington's latter years before considering the events leading up to the appearance of *Images of War*. Aldington's biography of T. E. Lawrence caused an unprecedented furor, and the ensuing widely expressed hostility was followed by the gradual disappearance of his work from bookshops and publishers' lists of reprints. There is no doubt that the literary and political establishment ganged up on Aldington for daring to expose "T. E. L. [as] a vainglorious liar who had fabricated his own legend at the expense of the real heroes of the Great War," and as a "national fraud."[29] All his life, apart from his three years' war service, Aldington could pride himself on having earned his living wholly from his writing. Now in the wake of the Lawrence controversy he was no longer able to do so. Without the generosity of two friends, Alister Kershaw and Bryher (Winifred Ellerman), Aldington would have had nowhere to live and no funds.[30] Aldington's stubborn and unwavering integrity throughout these final and problematic years has to be admired. Fred Crawford has charted the extraordinary obstacles that Aldington confronted when he challenged the T. E. Lawrence legend. Isolated, and in the face of various sources of hostility, Aldington saw his book through to publication, driven on by his "passion for the truth."[31] The result for Aldington in the aftermath of this controversy was personally and financially devastating. The result for the modern reader is the loss of a moving and important voice from the canon of British war writing.

∼

We can trace the publishing timetable of *Images of War* in Aldington's correspondence. The earliest reference occurs in a letter to Amy Lowell dated 2 January 1918. Aldington writes of his hopes and plans for publishing his war poems in a single volume. He is also at pains to distance his war poetry from the jingoistic, heroic mode of certain then-popular war poets. In addition Aldington makes explicit the cathartic effect he believes the publication of these poems would have for his own mental well-being. He says he has 60–70 war poems, but very different from the work of poets such as Rupert Brooke. He describes them as "bitter, anguish-stricken, realistic . . . stern truth." He says he has hesitated about publishing them, but that doing so would be a relief, a way of ridding himself of their clinging to him.[32]

The eventual publication of *Images of War* on both sides of the Atlantic in 1919 did not succeed, however, in entirely purging Aldington's mind and sensibility of his war experiences. They were to continue to resurface, and not only in the later prose works, *Death of a Hero* and *Roads to Glory*, but also in much of his verse throughout the 1920s and 1930s, and in the most unexpected places, for example in a number of the love poems in *Images of Desire*, in the ambitious long poem *A Fool i' the Forest: A Phantasmagoria*, and, finally, in the least likely context of all, in the lengthy narrative and subjective love poem, *A Dream in the Luxembourg*.

Some six months after his letter to Amy Lowell Aldington wrote to his wife, the poet H.D. (Hilda Doolittle), about his war poems. By this time (7 July 1918) he was able to inform her in some detail about the arrangements concerning the forthcoming publication of his war poems. The London publisher, C. W. Beaumont, had agreed to publish his war poems under the title *Images of War*, with accompanying illustrations by Paul Nash. It was to be a de luxe edition of two hundred, fifty of which would be colored by Nash himself. At this point Aldington had seen, and approved of, Nash's drawings for "Bombardment," "Barrage," "Dawn" and "Fatigues." Further drawings for other poems (seven, as it turned out) were in the process of being completed.[33]

In the event the war poems were not published until the following year. On 31 March 1919 Aldington wrote to Amy Lowell outlining for her benefit some details regarding the imminent publication of twenty-seven of his war poems. It was to be a limited edition of thirty copies on vellum, costing £1.10.0, fifty copies on fine paper, costing £1.1.0, and one hundred and twenty copies on ordinary paper, costing £0.12.0. Aldington was to receive just £15.0.0, but, as he pointed out, the copyright would be his after six months, and then he would be able to publish a cheap edition.[34] The appearance of this volume of Aldington's war poems was much enhanced by the cover and the eleven woodcuts executed by Paul Nash. In the thirty copies of the deluxe edition these woodcuts have been attractively watercolored by Nash, who also later designed and illustrated the covers for Aldington's *Death of a Hero* and *Roads to Glory*.

The subsequent Allen & Unwin edition of *Images of War*, published in December 1919, expanded the number of poems to forty-three, dropping three of the prose poems, and adding new poems. In June 1919 Elkin Mathews published *Images of Desire.* In September 1919 the Egoist Press published *Images,* a volume which combined both collections. Later in the same year a similar volume, *War and Love (1915–1918),* was published in America by the Four Seas Company.

One of the many positive early critical responses came from Harold Monro. Writing about *Images of War* in 1920, he was unstinting in his praise: "Except Siegfried Sassoon, no 'war-poet' has represented the torments of military life with such candour and so entirely without bombastic rhetoric."[35]

ALDINGTON'S WAR SERVICE

Influenced by the surge of patriotic feeling in the first months of the war, Aldington went to a local artillery armory, but was rejected by the inducting officer when he disclosed an earlier hernia operation. Throughout 1915 and the first part of 1916 the number of volunteers declined, and the second Military Act of May 1916 was introduced to boost the number of men serving in the armed forces. In late May Aldington and his friend Carl Fallas enlisted together in the 11th Battalion Devonshire Regiment. They were granted a few weeks to finalize their private affairs, and were eventually inducted into the army in late June to begin their war service as infantry privates at Worget Camp at Wareham in Dorset. H.D. followed him, living in the nearby village of Corfe Castle. After an initial period of training he moved in November to barracks at Verne Citadel on the Portland peninsula, following his transfer to the 11th Leicesters. He embarked for France on 21 December. After spending the last week of 1916 under canvas at a base camp near Calais, he served as a lance corporal in a Pioneer battalion on the Lens–La Bassée front, not far from Loos. Thus for the first few months of 1917 Aldington was employed in menial tasks of drudgery such as digging and repairing trenches, digging graves, and making crosses.

In July 1917 he returned to England for an officers' training course at Lichfield. While he was stationed there, H.D. lodged in a nearby hotel. Aldington received extensive training in signals and made rapid progress. He was commissioned as a Second Lieutenant in the 9th Battalion, the Royal Sussex Regiment on 28 November. After spending some time in camps at Newhaven and Tunbridge Wells undergoing further training in signals and technological work, he eventually joined his battalion in France on 8 April 1918. They were in the process of undergoing a spell of training before going north to St. Maroc, near Loos. On 6 June Aldington was sent on yet another training course.

By October his battalion was involved in the final "big push" to dislodge the Germans and drive them back. When the battalion signals officer became a casualty Aldington took over the role of signals and intelligence officer and was promoted to the rank of acting captain. On 4 November the 9th Royal Sussex took part in a massive assault on enemy positions on the Sambre Canal, where he was on 11 November. The Armistice did not bring early demobilization for Aldington, however. For him, as for many others, there was to be a protracted and frustrating delay before he could be released from his military duties.

The effect on Aldington of his three years of military service and the extent of the trauma he suffered during this period have been seriously underestimated, even travestied by unsympathetic commentators. Barbara Guest comments scornfully that Aldington's army experiences "had not been all that disagreeable. It is only necessary to compare [Death of a Hero] with Robert Graves' Goodbye to All That to realize that Aldington's experiences are not so desperate or tragic as he would have us believe." She adds, "the truth seems to be that he never fired a shot."[36] Surprisingly enough, even Aldington's biographer, Charles Doyle, appears to concur when he says that Guest's dismissive remark "is not entirely unfair."[37] In contrast, David Wilkinson presents detailed evidence to show that Aldington's war was "an experience more important and more personally challenging than the currently received accounts have generally suggested."[38] Zilboorg, too, confirms Aldington's damaged state of health, which continued well into the 1920s, that is, his bad nerves, attacks of boils, insomnia, the prolonged aftereffects of trench fever, and his psychological feelings of dislocation. She points out that "these . . . effects of the war were systemic and persisted for some time."[39] As late as 12 October 1925 Aldington wrote to Ezra Pound: "It is just three months since I got rid of the last boil on me [sic] back caused by drinking water full of corpses of several nations."[40]

It is perfectly true that in the course of these three years Aldington was remarkably fortunate to miss direct involvement in many of the major battles of the war. He was absent from the front line, either on leave or on training courses, during the most intense periods of fighting. It goes without saying that Aldington could not, and did not attempt to, manipulate matters so as to avoid battle conditions. Aldington himself was only too aware of his good fortune. On 16 July 1918 he wrote to H.D.: "My luck so far has been good. This is the fifth great battle I have just missed. I mustn't boast, though, lest I find myself in it this time tomorrow!"[41] Nevertheless, memories of his war experience remained powerful and vivid for decades after the event. For example, Aldington wrote to Count Geoffrey Potocki on 12 March 1959 to stress that he had been gassed, but not so seriously as to incapacitate him from military duties. He reminded Potocki that there is a description of being on the receiving end of German gas shelling in *Death of a Hero* (385–87). The gas in question was phosgene, not chlorine. Later he was to experience tear gas and "a whiff or two of mustard gas." Aldington says he cannot be certain that his bronchitis was a result of his being gassed.[42]

Later still, in a letter of 19 November 1958 to his friend Eric Warman, Aldington enclosed an evocative passage relating an incident in the autumn of 1918. Aldington had been sent down the line on a course intended to qualify him as a company commander. It was a rushed course since they had to rejoin their units as quickly as possible in order to take part in the long-awaited advance. The last part of their journey had to be made on foot, all available transport being required for the advance. They saw Cambrai and other towns and villages in flames. Aldington emphasizes that although he was writing some forty years later, he could vividly recall the sight of German cemeteries stretching as far as the eye could see. In addition they were surrounded by the desolation of war where nothing lived: the rats had been gassed, and the birds had died from drinking the foul water in shell holes. Wrecked guns, tanks, and vehicles lay strewn around, together with abandoned equipment: helmets, rifles, gas-masks, overcoats, and packs. Aldington was struck by the "utter silence . . . the utter desolation, the ugliness, the sense of misery, the regret of all our lost comrades."[43]

The titles of some of the final poems in *Images of War* give clear indications of Aldington's state of mind in the final months of the war, "Terror," "Defeat," "Doubt," "Resentment," and "Disdain," while "Apathy" reflects his mental condition in the immediate postwar period.

Indeed the end of the war did little to disperse these negative emotions. In *Life for Life's Sake* (published in 1941) Aldington recalls his involvement in the action of the final week of the war and his emotions in the immediate aftermath of the Armistice. Apart from some short-lived feelings of relief that it was finally all over, he was left with great sadness at the thought of such loss and waste, and anxiety about his own fractured life and about what the future held. He recalled the morning of 4 November. On this particular day his task was to move his men forward, while keeping battalion headquarters informed at regular intervals about his position. They passed through the German barrage with minimal losses, saw wounded and surrendering Germans going the other way, knocked out two machine-gun nests, advanced two miles, captured six guns, and took two hundred Germans prisoner. There followed another week of marching and seeing action against rear-guards before the Armistice arrived undramatically and undemonstratively. Aldington describes his emotions on this day as a confused mixture. He felt relieved, grateful, slightly hopeful, but deeply saddened. In addition he felt that his own inconsequential life, although spared, lay in ruins. (191–92)

Apart from the psychological and physical legacy of the war, Aldington's personal life did indeed appear to be in ruins. His relationship with H.D. was foundering; he had doubts about being able to write again; he could see no prospect of financial security in postwar England; and he feared he would be unable to resume his interrupted literary career.

On 12 November Aldington was suddenly and unexpectedly granted leave and began the long and irksomely slow journey back to England. He first had to hitchhike to Cambrai on a series of lorries through the endless desolation of ruined villages and the debris of war: collapsed trenches, wrecked guns and tanks, and vast amounts of equipment and belongings scattered and abandoned by the fleeing Germans. Aldington noticed that the attractive old Flemish houses, torched by the Germans before they left, still bore their beautiful carved Renaissance designs visible on the charred fragments. Aldington was also shocked by the way that the Germans had gratuitously defiled so many homes before they left. Eventually he is able to board a train that crawls slowly to Péronne, another ruined town, a tragic sight in its gaunt desolation. Aldington concludes this episode by remarking that the journey from the Franco-Belgian border to London took about eighty hours, and cites this as evidence of the confused and disorganized situation that succeeded the fighting. (192–95)

After this spell of leave Aldington returned to France in early December. It was at this time that he began to suffer from the aftereffects of what is loosely called "shell-shock," that is, a combination of nervous exhaustion, psychological disturbance and various physical ailments. He described some of these in *Life for Life's Sake*. He slept badly, was prone to inexplicable but unpleasant moods of depression, and was desperate to get out of the army. He felt that his mental powers had deteriorated, since he experienced great difficulty in concentrating on mental work. (195)

In addition Aldington began to chafe at the time-filling tasks he was given to occupy him in the post-Armistice period before the merciful release of demobilization. On 8 December he complained to Ezra Pound: "I am teaching Tommies to read the newspapers & do multiplication sums. . . . This education scheme is bullshit at its purest."[44] He finally received his demobilization papers in early February 1919 and on 8 February once more embarked on a near repeat of the trip he had made in the previous November. It was another extraordinary and uncomfortable journey, at first by mess cart through deep snow, then by rail, a slow, all-night journey in a windowless, doorless, unheated, unlit train. At dawn they reached Armentières, where they were given bowls of hot soup, and where those suffering from frostbite were evacuated to a hospital. (199) Aldington offered a few more details of his journey to England in a letter to Ezra Pound of 9 February. It entailed a twelve-hour ride in a frozen cattle truck. Aldington expected to catch a boat on 12 February, then, after reporting to the Crystal Palace, he hoped to be free to see Pound in London on 14 February. He was lucky not to have been held back for more months of military service as part of the army of occupation.[45]

Adjusting to civilian life once again was a painful experience for most returning soldiers. Not the least of their problems was attempting to make friends and relatives fully comprehend the effects of their war experiences. The myth of a suffering and traumatized élite who cannot fully communicate with, or be properly understood by, those who lack this particular experience is a leitmotiv that reappears constantly throughout the poetry, fiction, and memoirs of the Great War. In a letter to Clement Shorter[46] on 17 March 1919, Aldington expressed the problems he and many others like him faced. He questioned whether someone like Shorter could really appreciate the gulf that lay between those who fought and those who did not. Aldington found it a strain to make contact with these latter, feeling as if he were calling across a vast abyss that lay between him and them. He, together with all the other fighting men, had experienced misery, pain, hunger, despair, and death, while the noncombatants had lived, oblivious, in "favoured, comfortable England."[47]

Two weeks later he wrote to Amy Lowell to point out that she too had no conception of what the war had done to him. He held that she, as a noncombatant, was in no position to appreciate properly his physical and psychological problems. He listed for her his various complaints: bad nerves, neuralgia in his neck and arms, insomnia, and persistent sore throats and coughs. He admitted that all this sounded like a self-pitying whine, but that all of it was true. Finally he emphasized that none of the contents of this letter was to be passed on to H.D.[48]

Aldington had now been out of the war for over a year, and the aftermath would continue for some time. His mental and physical health would continue to cause problems, but these would ultimately diminish and gradually disappear. The bulk of his war poetry had been written, and by the end of the decade he would have added his prose works (*Death of a Hero* and *Roads to Glory*) in an attempt to exorcise once and for all the memories of war. In this he was not entirely successful, as the 1935 poem *Life Quest* testifies. In addition, there are also frequent references to the war in his later novels in the 1930s and in his correspondence with friends after the Second World War, e.g. in the 1958 letter to Eric Warman already referred to above.

ALDINGTON AND H.D.

Soon after his enforced premature departure from London University, Aldington worked part-time as a humble sports jour-

34

nalist and in his spare time was writing poetry and succeeding in getting some of his work published. At the same time he became involved with the London literary scene, where he made the acquaintance of some of the younger figures of the contemporary literary world, among them, significantly, two American expatriates, Ezra Pound and H.D. (Hilda Doolittle). The influence of Pound and H.D. was crucial in ensuring that Aldington was not to be linked with the dominant native English group of poets of the immediate prewar years, the Georgians, "regional in their outlook and in love with littleness,"[49] but to participate in the development of modernism in England.

~

Aldington's relationship with H.D. was important to him on both the personal and literary levels. They first met in late 1911 when he was twenty and she was twenty-six. Their relationship quickly blossomed when they realized that their reciprocal interest in each other was reinforced by the knowledge they were both practicing poets, professional colleagues in a literary movement, and that they shared many ideas and interests. In the summer of 1912 they went to Paris, where their mutual attraction was furthered by their joint literary and artistic passions.[50] On their return to London they were to participate in the birth of Imagism, and their poems were published in journals and anthologies on both sides of the Atlantic (see pp. 38–42).

This encouraging literary success was followed by their marriage on 18 October 1913. In *Life for Life's Sake* Aldington remains extremely reticent about their period together before marriage and about their life as a couple afterwards, but H.D.'s autobiographical novel, *Bid Me to Live* (not published until 1960), was, as she admitted, a *roman à clef,* so that we may perhaps read the characters of Rafe and Julia as substantially believable versions of Aldington and H.D.

The first two years of married life appear to have been happy and successful ones, both in terms of accomplishing important work and of laying the foundations of a stable loving relationship. Sadly, on 21 May 1915, H.D.'s pregnancy came to a tragic end with a stillborn child.[51] This traumatic event, together with Aldington's eventual participation in the war, proved to be crucial landmarks in their relationship. Both experiences were to be in some way responsible for their eventual separation. In February 1916 they moved from Hampstead to a north Devonshire cottage, where they continued to live until Aldington began his army service in June 1916.

Aldington and H.D. had agreed on an open marriage, but extramarital relationships produced tensions neither of them had foreseen. For example, Aldington's brief fling in May 1916 with Florence Fallas, the wife of his acquaintance, inevitably caused temporary problems in his own relationship with H.D.[52] Then in December 1917 he began an intense affair with Dorothy Yorke ("Arabella"). At this time she was occupying a room at the same address as H.D.'s flat at 44 Mecklenburgh Square in London. This relationship continued until Aldington ended it in 1928.[53] For her part H.D. became involved with the young musician and music critic, Cecil Gray, whom D. H. Lawrence and his wife Frieda had brought to her London flat. Gray fell in love with H.D. and invited her to go and live with him in Cornwall. She left London to go to Cornwall with Gray in April 1918, and one year later she gave birth to their child in April 1919.[54] Although these extramarital relationships meant that the Aldingtons' marriage was effectively over, they continued to correspond; in fact, they were not to divorce until 1938. This formal separation and the succeeding war years occasioned a break in their correspondence throughout the 1940s, but they were to renew their friendship and take up writing to each other on a regular basis once more after the Second World War.

Aldington's letters to H.D. during the First World War contain very little information about the war. He strove to minimize the horrors, to disguise his depression, and to conceal his anger and pessimism. However, in his letters to friends he disclosed more fully the details of the brutalizing experience of the early weeks of army life—the "bull," fatigues, and petty humiliations. For example, he enclosed the prose poem "Escape" (p. 146) in a letter to Bryher.[55] To H.D. he wrote about personal matters that concerned them, their relationship, their literary activities, and their efforts to get their work published. Occasionally, however, he gave way to the mood of despair that army experience frequently induced. In a letter to H.D. on 8 July 1918 he wrote about the deadening effect of the military existence and relieved his feelings with a satirical sketch of a visiting general. Life in the army often seemed to empty his mind, to dampen any glimmer of intelligence, to render everything dull and make him indifferent to everything. He put this down to the routine of army life and to the sweltering summer heat. In this context he describes their having to be inspected by a visiting general who gave a rousing pep talk, stressing the need to be active, efficient, and dutiful. Aldington characterized these necessary military qualities as being "everything that is contrary to us who worship thought, and freedom and reverie!"[56]

Occasionally, even in a letter substantially about literary matters, he could veer towards the harsh realities of war. In a letter to H.D. on 10 July 1918 Aldington wrote about some books he had sent her—by Samain, Gide, Renan, and Nietzsche. Referring to Nietzsche, he said that his preaching the individualism of 1840 to the communism of 1920 was out of date, inappropriate, and useless. A doctrine of common sense, not one of violence, was essential. Aldington would like to give Nietzsche a guided tour of the devastated town of Loos. This would be just one scene, representative of many, where "rats and lice [are] the sole benefactors of the superman ideal."[57]

In a letter of 13 October 1918 Aldington was anxious to reassure H.D. that although surrounded by death and devastation, he was nevertheless resilient and hoped to extract something beneficial from his experiences. Although surrounded by the usual detritus of the war—wrecked villages, a multitude of shell holes and wooden crosses—he found that his mind was tranquil and composed. He described his mood as one of acceptance, but not resignation. What was needed was to endure stoically and to apply what little wisdom one could muster in order to overcome the anguish and torment inflicted by others. On an unusually positive note he resolutely affirmed, "I feel ready for anything."[58]

By the time he wrote to H.D. on 14 October 1918 rumors of a possible end to hostilities seemed believable, and Aldington was starting to look forward to the prospect of returning to England and of attempting to reconstruct his life. He was, however, rather pessimistic about his future, saying, "It does not matter if I must hold out my hand for bread to my inferiors, if I must be beggar." He went on to urge H.D. to ignore and despise anyone talking of victory, to remember the countless dead, and to mourn them. In the future mankind had two prospects: it would either manage somehow to save itself from annihilation, or would allow greed, distrust, and malice to have a divisive effect.[59]

Glenn Hughes believes that Imagism was "the best-organized and most influential 'movement' in English poetry since the activity of the pre-Raphaelites."[60] During the immediate prewar period and the early part of the war several other groups, movements, and "isms" were likewise attempting to bring system and organization to their credo and to publicize their efforts. Vorticism, led by Wyndham Lewis, announced its manifesto through the belligerent pages of the two issues of *Blast* (June 1915 and July 1916). Marinetti's Futurists were also extremely active and vocal. The Vorticists were anxious to distance themselves from Marinetti's followers, and on Sunday 14 June 1914 a jointly signed letter to that effect appeared in the *Observer*. Aldington was one of those who signed this letter, along with Wyndham Lewis, Ezra Pound, David Bomberg, Henri Gaudier-Brzeska, and others. When the first issue of *Blast* appeared on 20 June, Aldington's name appeared once more among the signatories, a list of names almost identical to that under the *Observer* letter. At this time Aldington was also mixing with the likes of Edward Wadsworth, Ford Madox Hueffer (later to change his name to Ford Madox Ford), Violet Hunt, John Rodker, and Arthur Waley.[61]

H.D., who had known Pound in America, came to England in 1911. In London she met Aldington and they discovered that they both admired Greek poetry and the Hellenic tradition. In May 1912 she was in Paris with Aldington. Back in London in September they met up with Pound once again. Pound, as the representative and correspondent in England for *Poetry: A Magazine of Verse*, the magazine edited by Harriet Monroe in Chicago, sent some poems by H.D. and Aldington to Harriet Monroe. Under the contributions from H.D. he scribbled "H.D. Imagiste."[62] It was Pound who coined the term "Imagisme" (the word was later to lose its gallicized form) and who was instrumental in the publication of Imagist poems. In fact "Pound's initial leadership and shrewd critical judgment were indispensable to the founding of imagism as a real movement."[63] The first issue of Monroe's *Poetry* appeared in Chicago in October 1912. Monroe decided to print Aldington's poems in this first issue, and held back H.D.'s until the January 1913 issue. In his accompanying biographical notes Pound labels both Aldington and H.D. as "imagiste," but Aldington himself made light of the importance of the role he played in this poetic revolution. He explained how it came about that the poems of a nineteen-year-old English youth were first published in Chicago. There was no publishing outlet for such writing in England in 1912. Aldington happened to know Ezra Pound who was "busy . . . founding one of his biannual poetical 'movements',," but is at pains to play down his role in the so-called "revolution of 1912." By mere chance what he was then writing met with the approval of the "verse revolutionaries, just as the publication of the poems in America was an accident."[64]

The March 1913 issue of *Poetry* included F. S. Flint's three basic Imagist principles:

1. Direct treatment of the "thing," whether subjective or objective.
2. To use absolutely no word that does not contribute to the presentation.
3. As regards rhythm, to compose in sequence of the musical phrase, not in sequence of a metronome.

Pound's first Imagist anthology, in 1914, was bizarrely and ineptly titled *Des Imagistes*. It would seem that Pound's imperfect grasp of French prevented him from using the correct *Quelques Imagistes*, but soon after Pound abandoned the Imagists and moved on. "He sensed a slackening of dedication in the others, he was perhaps wise to depart for the more intensive Vorticism, which was a stricter form of Imagism.[65] It was gaining ground in its opposition to Futurism, which Pound described as a kind of "accelerated impressionism . . . a *spreading* or surface art."[66] Pound's letter to Monroe in January 1915 contains strictures about what he saw as a lack of rigor in certain contemporary poets, including some of the Imagists. These criticisms are couched in the terms of a school report, namely that Aldington has "occasional concentrations," that there are hints of promise, but that there is a "superficial cleverness" in him.[67] Concerning H.D. he gave a more positive assessment, referring to her "better emotional equipment," but without the "superficial cleverness" of Aldington. He anticipates she will "produce really fine things at great intervals."[68]

Three more anthologies followed in 1915, 1916, and 1917, now titled *Some Imagists*. They were edited by Amy Lowell in America, but mostly by Aldington in England. Amy Lowell's role in the Imagist movement was belittled by Pound when he coined the disparaging term "Amygism" for these subsequent Imagist anthologies. But her "diplomacy and patronage were essential to the continuance of the movement until it was firmly established."[69] However, Aldington and H.D. both agreed that much of Amy Lowell's own verse "was the fluid, fruity, facile stuff we most wanted to avoid. We wanted clear outlines, directness, concision, unhackneyed rhythms."[70] Lowell's 1915 anthology of Imagist poetry contained an unsigned preface that is substantially Aldington's. This key statement gives a clear and detailed exposition of the principles of the movement:

1. To use the language of common speech, but to employ always the exact word, not the nearly-exact, nor the merely decorative word.
2. To create new rhythms—as the expression of new moods— and not to copy old rhythms, which merely echo the old moods. We do not insist upon 'free verse' as the only method of writing poetry. We fight for it as for a principle of liberty. We believe that the individuality of a poet may often be better expressed in free verse than in conventional forms. In poetry, a new cadence means a new idea.
3. To allow absolute freedom in the choice of subject. It is not good art to write badly about aeroplanes and automobiles; nor is it necessarily bad art to write well about the past. We believe passionately in the artistic value of modern life, but we wish to point out that there is nothing so uninspiring nor so old-fashioned as an aeroplane of the year 1911.
4. To present an image (hence the name, imagist). We are not a school of painters, but we believe that poetry should render particulars exactly and not deal in vague generalities, however magnificent and sonorous. It is for this reason that we oppose the cosmic poet, who seems to us to shirk the real difficulties of his art.
5. To produce poetry that is hard and clear, never blurred nor indefinite.

6. Finally, most of us believe that concentration is of the very essence of poetry.[71]

Assessments of H.D.'s early poetry have tended to concentrate on her purely as an Imagist. In his study of the Imagist movement Glenn Hughes characterizes Aldington as "The Rebel," and H.D. as "The Perfect Imagist."[72] Richard E. Smith repeats this evaluation of H.D.: "H.D.'s poems have been generally recognized as the most perfect productions of the imagists."[73] Cyrena Pondrom, however, using "Hermes of the Ways" as a key example, has convincingly demonstrated that this view of H.D.'s poetry is too limiting and constrictive. She argues that H.D. is far more substantial than is generally acknowledged by most literary historians; that she played a significant role not only in the founding of one strain of modernist poetry, but also made a major contribution "to the development of the dynamic current of modernism which shaped the nature of a literary generation and beyond."[74]

To return to H.D.'s Imagist poetry, two examples, both from the 1915 anthology *Some Imagist Poets,* display the qualities of her skillfully wrought poetry. These are "Oread," and "The Garden." The expressive power of these poems results not only from their clarity, intensity and economy. In them H.D. deploys a series of verbs for their *dynamic* qualities: "whirl," "splash," and "hurl," in the first, and "rend," "cut," and "plough,"in the second.

In a letter to Amy Lowell in November 1917 Aldington declared that "H. D.'s poetry is the only modern English poetry I really care for. Its austerity, its aloofness, its profound passion for that beauty which only Platonists know, make it precisely the kind of work I would like to do myself, had I the talent."[75] Years later, in *Life for Life's Sake*, Aldington continued to speak in glowing terms of H.D.'s aesthetic sensibility and of her poetic strengths. He rates her as more distinguished than Ezra Pound, superior both as a person and in her mind. No one possessed a more vivid aesthetic sensibility, or a more original and sensitive intelligence. In her poetry she conveyed a passionate meditation of beauty. (111) Aldington was in awe of the strict self-criticism she displayed as she sought perfection, at the way she ruthlessly pruned her work so as to achieve such flawless craftsmanship. (138) Aldington also claims that for a time even D. H. Lawrence was influenced by H.D. (140)

Imagism came to an end as a coherent and self-contained movement in 1917. Aldington informs us in *Life for Life's Sake* that the involvement of America in the war in 1917 caused Amy Lowell to decide that they should all go their own ways (143). In addition, Aldington's military service meant that he was unable to continue with editorial responsibilities. There was, however, to be one final Imagist flourish. Following up a semiserious suggestion, Aldington set to work to edit a final anthology, and so, with the assistance of Ford Madox Ford and H.D., Imagism signed off with the *Imagist Anthology, 1930*. The only names missing from the list of previous participants and contributors were Amy Lowell, who had died in 1925, and Ezra Pound, who was "sulky."[76] Pound had refused to cooperate with or participate in any ventures by the original Imagist poets after 1914.

The position occupied by Imagism in twentieth century literature and the extent of its useful influence has been succinctly and appositely summed up by Herbert Read. Read saw Imagism as too limited in its details and scope to survive as a poetic movement, but felt that it had been a necessary phenomenon in the development of English poetry. Aldington, H.D., and F. S. Flint had a cleansing influence on the literary atmosphere between 1910 and 1915. In so doing, they had helped prepare the ground for Pound and T. S. Eliot.[77]

CONCLUSION

The presence of Richard Aldington's name, heading, in alphabetical order, those of Laurence Binyon, Edmund Blunden, Rupert Brooke, W. W. Gibson, Robert Graves, Julian Grenfell, Ivor Gurney, David Jones, Robert Nichols, Wilfred Owen, Herbert Read, Isaac Rosenberg, Siegfried Sassoon, Charles Sorley, and Edward Thomas on the memorial to the poets of the First World War in Westminster Abbey, gives some indication of his true stature. This first collection of his war poetry should lead to a long overdue reevaluation and a new appreciation of his significant contribution to the literature of the Great War, and of his literary worth. Perhaps we can look forward as well to the republication of *Death of a Hero*.

During his lifetime the most important official recognition of Aldington came from the Soviet Union where his work was widely published, read, and valued. In 1962 he accepted an invitation from the Union of Writers of the USSR to spend three weeks in June–July as their honored guest.

A few months before leaving for Russia, Aldington wrote to his friend Lawrence Durrell on 15 March 1962. In this letter he explains why he had refused to accept another invitation to appear on television. It was to take part in a program about soldier-writers of both world wars, or, as Aldington put it, "the two fracas." The other participants (whom he does not identify) he termed "chair-borne warriors of the knife-and-fork brigade, BBC war embusqués who wept for the soldier at a guinea a tear." Aldington considered it a "blasted cheek" to be asked to "bolster those bastards." He explained how his thoughts then returned to the Somme battlefields, to the detritus of war, to the chaos of graves, to the burning towns, to the slow journeys in freezing trains, and to the "tragical desolation of death. You can't make a show of such memories."[78]

Soon after his return from Russia, where he had been belatedly fêted and lionized, Aldington died of a heart attack on 27 July 1962 in his home at Sury-en-Vaux. He was seventy years old.

In an eloquent tribute to Aldington on 1 August 1987, his old friend, Alistair Kershaw stressed

> his generous enthusiasms, his love of life, his capacity for absolute and unquestioning devotion, his readiness, his eagerness to help his fellow writers—F. S. Flint, Remy de Gourmont, T. S. Eliot, André Spire, and yes, most of all, H.D. to whom Richard gave throughout his whole life his admiration, his devotion, his consideration and tenderness.[79]

Early Poems

The small group of poems in this section illustrates two of the four broad themes that recur throughout Aldington's verse, namely, his Hellenism and his response to the society in which he lived. The third and fourth strands, love of woman, and love of the natural world, can be traced in many of the later poems, including the war poems.

May Sinclair "saw in Aldington a split personality: one half a poet of classical Greece and the other half a poet of modern times."[80] She felt "it was the Greek Richard Aldington who ripened to a precocious mastery; the modern poet that is no less surely in him has not even approached maturity." [81] This distinction can be substantiated when considering some of the poems in this section. The Greek side of Aldington is dominant and fully realized in "Fantasy" and "Captive." In both poems the war is treated obliquely and implicitly. McGreevy sees "Captive" as a farewell "to all the dream of loveliness of the young poet," and to the "boyish dream of Greek serenity," something which does not exist except as part of an artist's created reality. The donning of military uniform would make all this classical idealism seem even more unreal and irretrievable.[82]

Another reviewer identified the same unresolved dichotomy, expressing the hope that "Mr. Aldington will complete the story with a satisfying resolution of his Arcadian-modernistic discord."[83]

"Sunsets," "Hampstead Heath," and "London" concentrate simply upon providing tantalizing glimpses of the modern world. Indeed, the first six lines of "Sunsets" have the vividness and terseness typical of much Imagist verse. The war impinges on London as a barely perceptible, but nevertheless, ominous threat. McGreevy notes that it "is a poet's reaction, expressed in brutal images, away from the dream and towards the new reality."[84]

"Hampstead Heath" captures in impressionistic touches the hectic bustle of Bank Holiday pleasure seekers, while overhead searchlight beams sweep the dark clouds for possible threat from the air.

"London" is similarly impressionistic, with the concision of each two or three-line stanza possibly suggesting the influence of the Japanese *haiku*. In the final five lines the poet/speaker expresses his fear that all this natural and man-made beauty might be annihilated in war. The unidentified aerial threat— zeppelins—hinted at in "Hampstead Heath" and "London," is spelled out in a letter of 14 September 1915 to F. S. Flint. He told how for fifteen minutes there was shrapnel bursting overhead, that he saw the Zeppelin, and wondered what its next target might be. He listed the various London landmarks that had been hit. These included Harold Monro's Poetry Bookshop. He described it as having been the most serious air raid up till then.[85]

"Sloane Street" contrasts various sources of light—moon, searchlight and stars—high above, with the ground-level gloom of a wartime London reduced to severely restricted lighting. The first stanza's clear visualization of these light sources is followed by the second stanza's paradox of war, giving Londoners the opportunity to appreciate more profoundly the beauty of the night sky.

"A Life" contains enough circumstantial detail to identify the unnamed young artist as Aldington's friend, the precociously gifted French sculptor, Henri Gaudier-Brzeska[86]: his poverty, his indifference to material comforts, personal hygiene and social niceties, his flippant attitude to life except where his art was concerned, his integrity, and finally his premature death in the war. In his autobiography Aldington describes Gaudier-Brzeska as "probably the dirtiest human being I have ever known . . . [he] gave off horrid effluvia in hot weather." Aldington relates how one hot summer day when Gaudier-Brzeska came to visit he was relegated to one end of the room while the rest of the company retired to the other. Aldington also points out that in his lifetime Gaudier made very little money out of his work. (165–67). Ezra Pound observed a fundamental but finally amicable disagreement in matters of artistic tradition between Aldington and Gaudier-Brzeska, the former a defender of the values and achievement of Greek civilization and culture, the latter a vociferous advocate of primitivism.[87]

NOTES

1. Gates, 1992, 127.
2. Ibid., 109.
3. Ibid., 314.
4. Dyer, 1995, 78.
5. Hynes, 1990, 425.
6. Eksteins, 1989, 290–91.
7. Gates, 1992, 140.
8. Aldington's subsequent formal education at University College, London, was cut short since he was forced to abandon his studies there because his father was unable to continue to pay his fees.

9. Gates, 1992, 27–28.

10. One action of Nevill's provides an odd footnote to military history. On 1 July 1916, the first day of the Battle of the Somme, he made the eccentric, yet somehow typical, decision to issue a football to each of his four platoons. The twenty-two-year-old Nevill offered a prize to the first platoon to reach the German lines dribbling their football (he was himself killed soon after going over the top, and is buried in Carnoy Military Cemetery). Two of the footballs that featured in this memorable act of foolish bravado have survived. One is in the National Army Museum, London, the other in the Queen's Regiment Museum, Canterbury.

11. Tylee, 1990, 237.

12. Parfitt, 1988, 43–65.

13. Bergonzi, 1965, 185–86.

14. For example, Maxim Gorky, Arnold Bennett, H. G. Wells, Lawrence Durrell, C. P. Snow, and Anthony Burgess.

15. McGreevy, 1931, 56 and 61.

16. John Morris, "Richard Aldington and *Death of a Hero* or Life of an Antihero?" in Klein, 1978, 185.

17. Tate, 1998, 82.

18. Taylor, 1989, 29.

19. Khan, 1994, 106–7.

20. Cadogan & Craig, 1978, 88.

21. McGreevy, 1931, 33.

22. Caroline Zilboorg, "H.D.'s Influence on Richard Aldington," in Doyle, 1990, 36.

23. David Wilkinson, *Roads to Glory*. London: Imperial War Museum, 1992, viii. This is a limited facsimile edition of three hundred copies of the first edition, together with a reproduction of Paul Nash's original cover.

24. We should note that most of the profane language that adds authenticity to the soldiers' speech in this part of the novel was expunged from the original 1929 edition, and not reinstated until 1965.

25. *Reverie: A Little Book of Poems for H.D.* was published in 1917. One of the key poems of *Images of War* is entitled "Reverie."

26. Zilboorg, 1992, 77–79.

27. Barlow, 1995.

28. MacNiven & Moore, 1981, xiv.

29. Crawford, 1998, 12.

30. Ibid., 201.

31. Ibid., 206.

32. Gates, 1992, 30.

33. Zilboorg, 1992, 93.

34. Gates, 1992, 47.

35. Monro, 1920, 99.

36. Guest, 1984, 85–86.

37. Doyle, 1989, 60.

38. David Wilkinson, " 'Dying at the Word of Command': The Last Days of Richard Aldington's War," in Blayac & Zilboorg, 1995, 7.

39. Zilboorg, 1992, 201.

40. Ibid., 201.

41. Ibid., 108.

42. Gates, 1992, 294–95.

43. Zilboorg, 1992, 146–47.

44. Ibid., 164.

45. Ibid., 189.

46. The founder and editor of *The Sphere*, a weekly publication for which Aldington wrote nine articles between April and October 1919.

47. Zilboorg, 1992, 201.

48. Gates, 1992, 47.

49. *Life for Life's Sake*, 110.

50. Zilboorg, 1992, 51.

51. Doyle, 1989, 40–42

52. Guest, 1984, 78.

53. Zilboorg, 1992, 227.

54. Guest, 1984, 88–90, 93–97.

55. Winifred Ellerman, the writer, whom H.D. first met in 1918. The two women remained lifelong and intimate friends.

56. Zilboorg, 1992, 97.

57. Ibid., 104.

58. Ibid., 146.

59. Ibid., 148.

60. Hughes, 1931, vii.

61. Wadsworth, 1989, 65.

62. H.D., *End to Torment: A Memoir of Ezra Pound*, ed. Norman Holmes Pearson & Michael King. New York: New Directions, 1979, 18.

63. Smith, 1977, 41.

64. *The Complete Poems of Richard Aldington*, 1948, 13.

65. The Vorticists were certainly vociferous in their touting of their work as such.

66. Jones, 1972, 21.

67. Ibid., 142.

68. Ibid., 142.

69. Smith, 1977, 41.

70. *Life for Life's Sake*, 137.

71. Amy Lowell (ed.), *Some Imagist Poets: An Anthology*, 1915, vi–vii.

72. Hughes, 1931, 11.

73. Smith, 1977, 41.

74. Cyrena N. Pondrom, "H.D. and the Origins of Imagism," in Friedman and DuPlessis, 1990, 96–99.

75. Gates, 1998, 28–29.

76. Aldington, 1968, 131.

77. Kershaw & Temple, 1965, 132.

78. MacNiven & Moore, 1981, 209.

79. Gates, 1992, 220.

80. Gates, 1974, 6.

81. "The Poems of Richard Aldington," *The English Review*, Vol. 32, No. 5 (May 1921), 397–410. Gates, 1974, 7.

82. McGreevy, 1931, 26.

83. Paul F. Baum, "Mr. Richard Aldington," *South Atlantic Quarterly*, Vol. 28, No. 2 (April 1929), 201–8. Gates, 1974, 7.

84. McGreevy, 1931, 27.

85. Gates, 1992, 18.

86. Gaudier-Brzeska's work was an eclectic and energetic amalgam of prim-

itivism and Cubism. In spite of his early death in the war at the age of twenty-three his reputation has grown steadily, and the importance of his place in the development of modernist sculpture in Britain in the early part of the twentieth century is assured.

87. Pound, 1960, 30.

Part I
Early Poems

Sunsets

The white body of the evening
Is torn into scarlet,
Slashed and gouged and seared
Into crimson,
And hung ironically
With garlands of mist.

And the wind
Blowing over London from Flanders
Has a bitter taste.

[*The Anglo-French Review,* 1916; *Some Imagist Poets,* 1916]

Hampstead Heath

(Easter Monday, 1915)

Dark clouds, torn into gaps of livid sky,
Pierced through
By a swift searchlight, a long white dagger.
The black murmuring crowd
Flows, eddies, stops, flows on
Between the lights
And the banks of noisy booths.

[*Images (1910–1915),* 1915; *Images Old and New,* 1916]

London

May 1915

Glittering leaves
Dance in a squall;
Behind them bleak immoveable clouds.

A church spire
Holds up a little brass cock
To peck at the blue wheat fields.

Roofs, conical spires, tapering chimneys,
Livid with sunlight, lace the horizon.

A pear-tree, a broken white pyramid
In a dingy garden, troubles me
With ecstasy.

At night, the moon, a pregnant woman,
Walks cautiously over the slippery heavens.

And I am tormented,
Obsessed,
Among all this beauty,
With a vision of ruins,
Of walls crumbling into clay.

[*Images (1910–1915)*, 1915; *Images Old and New, 1916*]

Fantasy

The limbs of gods,
Still, veined marble,
Rest heavily in sleep
Under a saffron twilight.

Not for them battle,
Severed limbs, death, and a cry of victory;

Not for them strife
And a torment of storm.

A vast breast moves slowly,
The great thighs shift,
The stone eyelids rise;
The slow tongue speaks:

'Only a rain of bright dust
In the outer air;
A little whisper of wind;
Sleep; rest; forget.'

Bright dust of battle!
A little whisper of dead souls!

[*The Anglo-French Review*, 1916, entitled "1915"]

Sloane Street

I walk the streets and squares
Of this lampless war-time London,
Beautiful in its dusk.
On the right an orange moon;
On the left a searchlight,
A silver stream among the stars.

London was a rich young man
Burdened with great possessions—
Now, poor in light,
Menaced, and a little frightened,
At length he sees the stars.

[*The Egoist*, Vol. 3, No. 3 (1 March
1916), p. 39. Gates, 1974, 253.]

A Life

He was a peasant boy
With sharp eyes and beaked nose;
His hair was too long, ragged
And a little greasy.

He was generous, indifferent to comforts,
Lived on bread, onions and apples—
Worked in a shed under a railway arch—
Was very witty and a little violent.
His red shirt was none too clean;
When he got hot he stank.
His hands were mostly filthy
With marble-dust and clay.

In all his sketches and statues
He made you see something fresh—
An unsuspected beauty, a new strength,
The clear line of a naked woman's body,
The lightness of a stag,
A new grotesqueness or hideousness.

He had the blithe intolerance of the very young
But there was nothing petty in him;
He worked hard, had no obvious vices.

Then the war came.
He went off with a joke:
"I'll be back safe in three months:
I'll steal the Picassos from Düsseldorf!"

He was away three months
And another three months;
Was wounded, promoted, went back,
Accepted things cheerfully,
"Without arrogance" (his own phrase).

A few more weeks—
He was shot in the head.
Quenched that keen, bright wit,

Horribly crushed the wide forehead,
Limp and useless the able hands
Of our one young sculptor.
I wish he were not dead;
He was wholesome, his dirt and his genius.
So many "artists" are muffs, poseurs, pifflers.

I sit here, cursing over my Greek—
Anacreon says:
"War spares the bad, not the good."

I believe him.

[*The Egoist*, Vol. 3, No. 5 (1 May 1916), p. 69. Gates, 1974, 257–58. The sculptor in question is Henri Gaudier-Brzeska, who was killed on 5 June 1915 during an attack on Neuville St. Vaast.]

Captive

They have torn the gold tettinx
From my hair;
And wrenched the bronze sandals
From my ankles.

They have taken from me my friend
Who knew the holy wisdom of poets,
Who had drunk at the feast
Where Simonides sang.

No more do I walk the calm gardens
In the white mist of olives;
No more do I take the rose-crown
From the white hands of a maiden.

I, who was free, am a slave;
The Muses have forgotten me,
The gods do not hear me.
Here there are no flowers to love;

But afar off I dream that I see
Bent poppies and the deathless asphodel.

[*The Anglo-French Review*, 1917]

IMAGES OF WAR

Reverie: A Little Book of Poems for H.D. was published in 1917 by The Clerk's Press in Cleveland, Ohio. It consists of just nine poems, seven of which were included in *Images of War* in its final form. These are "Proem," "Reverie," "The Wine Cup" "Ananke," "Disdain," "An Earth Goddess," and "Epilogue." The remaining two, "Sorcery of Words" and "Our Hands," both prose poems, were to appear in 1926 in *The Love of Myrrhine and Konallis, and Other Prose Poems*. All nine are included in the present volume, with the latter two in the Prose Poems section.

"Reverie," the title poem of the small booklet, is one of the longest in *Images of War*. It is rarely anthologized, yet it is one of Aldington's central war poems. In measured tones he successfully interweaves three of his core threads: a realistic depiction of the war, his love of nature, and his love of woman. The first four lines establish the discomfort and danger of the trenches: "It is very hot in the chalk trench / With its rusty iron pickets / And shell-smashed crumbling traverses, / Very hot and choking and full of evil smells." Moving into his dug-out, the poet is unable to find the solitude he seeks and needs. Mundane military matters invade his privacy: "How many billets have we in such a trench?" and "Do you know the way to such a redoubt?" But the strength of the poet's love is such that, in the second stanza, it temporarily erases the misery of his present existence. Now the choking heat of the trenches is replaced by an inner heat: "I am burned with a sweet madness, / Soothed also by the fire that burns me." Vivid memories of their last physical contact sustain him, and although the war interrupts his reverie yet again ("the hot sun burns in the white trench / And the shells go shrilling overhead / And I am harassed by stupid questions"), nevertheless they are weaker than his mental reconstruction of their love: "I do not forget to build dreams of her." The poet lists various reasons for existing—religion, patriotism, financial reward, political power or adherence to a cause—but he relegates them

56

to an inferior position compared with his love. Death or mutilation may await him, but he is convinced that their love will survive, even though the evidence of "dead men lying on the earth / Or carried slowly in stretchers" carries a powerfully contrary message. The poet wishes for their mutual death, that they might be together in some pagan paradise with "no memory of this fret of life." He imagines her stooping to pick a flower, a symbol of their love. No words are exchanged; there is no need to express their love through speech. But the war irrupts once more: "The guns are beating madly upon the still air / With sudden rapid blows of sound, / And men die with the quiet sun above them / And horror and pain and noise upon earth." The last stanza pulls all the threads together. The poet knows full well that death on the battlefield is a likely outcome, but, strengthened by his dream construct, he, together with his beloved and "the pale flower," the symbol of their love, are "together in a land of quiet / Inviolable behind the walls of death." In fact, Susan Stanford Friedman describes the poems in *Reverie* as " 'madrigals,' modernist style, their pastoral passions mediated by the historical realities of war," poems that alternate "between images of anguish and images of a redemptive desire."[88]

In its final form *Images of War* is a carefully planned and clearly structured entity. Between the framing poems, "Proem" and "Epilogue," there are three chronologically ordered groups. The first poems cover leaving civilian life and the period of early training. These are followed by a long sequence of poems that treat the physical and psychological aspects of front-line experience. Finally, a small group of poems deal with the problematic return to civilian life and the difficulty of adjustment to the postwar world.

In "Proem" Aldington alludes to the dilemma that Ivor Gurney addressed in "War Books": "What did they expect of our toil and extreme / Hunger—the perfect drawing of a heart's dream? / Did they look for a book of wrought art's perfection . . . ?" Aldington asserts that in the chaos of war he cannot find the tranquil certainties that he formerly derived from the Greek gods. The "austere shape" eludes him. He feels powerless to create artistic form out of the disorder of war.

In "Vicarious Atonement" he takes this search for compensatory meaning a step further. He believes that if out of the loss and waste of war some poetic achievement proves to be possible then he and others "can endure." Nevertheless, the poet still prays to the "old and very cruel god" (of war?) to relieve their suffering: "Take, if thou will, this bitter cup from us."

In "Leave-Taking" the war is menacingly present, although there is no direct reference to it. The poem's main point is to wonder whether the consolatory beauties of the natural world will continue to exist for the loved one if and when the soldier-poet is killed. Ominously the poppy might "spout blood," the five petals of the campion might symbolize the extinction of the five senses, and the sea might turn "stale."

"Bondage" is a meditation contrasting past happiness and prodigality in lines 1–18 with, in lines 19–33, what the soldier-poet experiences in his early days in uniform. He inhabits an ugly, barren world: "There are no leaves, no sea, / No shade of a rich orchard, / Only a sterile dusty waste, / Empty and threatening." He has lost his former freedoms of both mind and body: "I long vainly for solitude, / And the lapse of silent hours; / I am frantic to throw off / My heavy cloth and leather garments, / To set free my feet and body." The only consolations he can find are banal and meager ones, but they are important: "A yellow daisy seems to clutch my heart," and "I am grateful even to humility / For the taste of pure clean bread."

In "Field Manoeuvres: Outpost Duty" the poet is lying down, not in the trenches yet, but on maneuvers as part of his training somewhere in England. His senses are finely tuned, at first to what is close at hand, to the damp earth, to the smell of grass and woodland. Raising his head slightly he sees a shining stretch of roadway. Looking up he sees the cloud masses in the sky. At this point Aldington introduces an original and surprising image. The clouds are presented as "interminable squadrons of silver and blue horses" that "Pace in long ranks the blank fields of heaven." The military connotations of "squadrons" and "ranks" are nevertheless appropriate in this context. After touch, smell, and sight comes hearing. Just three delicate natural sounds are audible. "There is no sound" means there is no unnatural man-made sound to invade this silence. The poet's reverie is interrupted by his recalling the instructions he received before being posted on the edge of the wood, namely that he was "to fire at the enemy column / After it has passed." But instead of holding his rifle as instructed he has allowed it to lie on the ground. The poet's inner private self has separated from his military self and he responds ecstatically to the natural beauty around him.

"Dawn" begins the long sequence of poems charting the authentic experience of war. Nature is no longer the consolatory presence of "Field Manoeuvres." Instead "grim dawn," "bleak clouds," "flooded meadows," and a "death-pale, death-still mist" set the scene, matched by the exhaustion of the troops. Just as the men's "pretence of gaiety" fools no one, least of all themselves, so the rising sun brings deceptive color to the sky. This short poem is skillfully structured around a series of contrasts and repetitions. The counterweight to the red sky of dawn is the "black and aching anguish" in the men's hearts. Their silent wish is for an end to this torment, that the "crimson" in the sky will be echoed in their blood, the "vivid crimson agonies of death." At the end of the poem we come full circle. The reality of the "death-pale, death-still mist" will lift, to be replaced by death in the metaphorical shape of a "mist-pale sleep."

In "The Lover" the lover whom the poet yearns for is not a woman in some Edenic garden, "In the time of soft-plum blossoms / When the air is gay with birds singing." Rather she is a personification of violent death, one who "will clutch me with fierce arms / And stab me with a kiss like a wound / That bleeds slowly." But the initial pain will disappear and she will bring him peace and rest. Sassoon also uses the trope of love as a prelude to death in his poem "The Kiss." Whereas Sassoon's kiss is that of the bayonet he imagines himself plunging into an enemy soldier's body, Aldington's kiss is passively received without any explicit reference to the agency of a German soldier.

"A Moment's Interlude" allows the poet to escape from the war and to immerse himself in and to blend with a sanative, consolatory nature. Natural forms are personified as welcoming presences: "Bracken fronds beckoned from the darkness / With exquisite frail green fingers," and "The tree-gods muttered affectionately about me." Even an oblique reference to the war cannot break the charm: "And from the distance came the grumble of a kindly train." In the final stanza the poet's sense of bliss leads him to imagine his body and the earth conjoined in some kind of mystical congress: "I could have laid my cheek in the grasses / And caressed with my lips the hard sinewy body / Of Earth, the cherishing mistress of bitter lovers."

In "On the March" the poet's ecstatic response to nature as he marches along leads him to liken the red berries to the nipples of a girl's breasts. He imagines himself free of all his burdensome military impedimenta and able to frolic naked. He would be able to write poems about "the women of Hellas," the "rent seas," and "the peace of olive gardens." The poet also envisages writing poems about the here and now, about "these rough meadows," and even about "the keen welcome smell of London mud!" Just at the moment of celebration of this imagined freedom the words of command bring him brutally back to earth: "Party—HALT!"

In the first three lines of "In the Trenches" the poet asserts that he and his fellow soldiers can cope with exhaustion, fear, and loneliness; he differentiates being lonely from being alone. He then goes on to say that the wounds suffered by the earth are shared by men as well. Not only are their bodies broken but their minds and nerves are equally shattered. The mortars, bullets and shells "Sever and rend the fine fabric / Of the wings of our frail souls, / Scatter into dust the bright wings / Of Psyche!" This reference to a specific Greek myth works very effectively here as a complex multi-layered image. "Psyche" in Greek signifies both "soul" and "butterfly." In works of art Psyche is often represented as a maiden with the wings of a butterfly. The destructive ordnance of war threatens the soldier's spiritual life, as much as it does his material existence. There is a third implicit reading of this image. Many soldiers in the trenches noted the paradoxical presence of butterflies whose fragility and beauty were also threatened by bullets and shells. The line "Scatter into dust the bright wings" has a powerful visual quality and describes precisely what would happen should a bullet hit a butterfly. In the second part of the poem the poet is comforted by the thought that all this destruction is powerless to effect permanent change in nature. The moon and the stars will continue to appear in the sky, the hard earth will be broken up by the action of frost, and flowers will bloom again each spring. Aldington moves effortlessly from the lofty and remote heights to a harsh, down-to-earth reality, both in terms of subject matter and language. On the one hand we have "the moon / Haughty and perfect," "the Pleiades," "Orion," and "patient creeping stalk and leaf"; on the other we have "barren lines," "huge rats," "the hawk," and "the carrion crow." After the rhetorical question "Can you stay them with your noise?" the poet defiantly challenges the war machine to do the impossible: "Then kill winter with your cannon, / Hold back Orion with your bayonets / And crush the spring leaf with your armies!"

The narrative of the poem "Trench Idyll" is conveyed at first in indirect speech as the narrator summarises the conversation he has had with a fellow officer as they reminisced about London's social pleasures. This is followed by a section of dialogue. In flat, realistic language, using the rhythms of everyday speech, the senior and more experienced officer describes the one death he has witnessed at the front. He then continues with a description of how he had to collect the identity discs from the badly decomposed bodies of men who had been hanging on the barbed wire for six months. In this dialogue there is a marked contrast between the matter-of-fact narrative of the senior officer and the brief responses of the junior officer who feels obliged to interject some comment from time to time. The inadequacy and banality of his feeble clichés serve to underline the ghastliness of the incidents being recounted to him: "That's odd," "Good Lord, how terrible!", and "It's rather cold here, sir, suppose we move?"

At the start of "A Village" the poet recalls how he used to dismiss his home village back in England as "flat and commonplace," but, standing in a trench during a lull in the fighting, he realizes the importance of apparently banal and ordinary sights: "What a tree means, what a pool, / Or a black wet field in sunlight." In the third and fourth sections the poet lists the aspects of the nearby French village he has learned to love and value. The poet loves even the pathetic village church, "The poorest ever built, I think," in spite of its unrefined qualities. It is here that Aldington brings his aesthetic sensibility to bear upon the church's stylistic shortcomings: "With all its painted plaster saints / Straight from the Rue St. Sulpice, / Its dreadful painted windows, / And Renaissance "St. Jacques le Majeur" / Over the porch." In the final section the poet enjoys a short respite some way back from the front line and revels in the "rich life" of "this poor drab village" which he insists is as beautiful as Florence or Damascus.

The first stanza of "Machine Guns" conveys the visual impression of bullets ricocheting off stones: "gold flashes," and "Gold sparks." The vividness of this image contrasts with the indistinct scene of the second stanza in which men are depicted occupying the bottom of a trench. One is lying wounded, being tended by stretcher-bearers. Nearby is an anonymous huddled mass of soldiers: "And at our feet / Cower shrinkingly against the ground / Dark shadowy forms of men." In the third stanza Aldington abandons the visual and the descriptive for an ironic comment on the expectations placed upon him and a fellow officer. They are not supposed to cower in the trenches and thereby set a bad example for the men: "Only we two stand upright." Their different backgrounds and personalities have disappeared behind this joint façade of cool disregard to danger: "All differences of life and character smoothed out / And nothing left / Save that one foolish tie of caste / That will not let us shrink."

"Three Little Girls" is a rare occurrence ("April Lieder" is the only other example in *Images of War)* of Aldington's abandoning *vers libre* for a more regular verse form. Here he alternates tetrameters with dimeters. Smith plausibly suggests that in this instance Aldington has departed from his more usual free verse "in his compassion for the innocent martyrs to the vicissitudes of war."[89] Towards the end the poem veers ever so slightly towards the sentimental with "Three little girls with names of saints / And angels' eyes." However, the earlier realistic touches of "broken shoes / And hard sharp coughs," and the fact that they "sold us sweets too near the shells" give us glimpses of civilian hardship and damaged childhood occasioned by the proximity of war.

"Soliloquy–1" begins with a declaration of bravery, but one with reservations: "No. I'm not afraid of death / (Not very much afraid, that is) / Either for others or myself." The poet has grown accustomed to seeing stretchers bringing in the wounded. He tries to carry on as normal, having a bite to eat and even joking. At the end of the first part the poet refers to each corpse as "it." In the second part he admits that his equanimity is not secure against an emotional response: "The way they wobble!—/ God! that makes one sick." In death man should still retain his dignity: "Dead men should be so still, austere, / And beautiful, / Not wobbling carrion roped upon a cart." There comes a time when jokes are a wholly inadequate as well as inappropriate reaction to such horrors. The separate final line has a laconic quality, a device often used to good effect by Siegfried Sassoon: "Well, thank God for rum."

"Soliloquy–2" is in effect a paired poem with "Soliloquy–1." The poet contradicts his earlier description of corpses as "carrion." He relates an incident when he and some fellow soldiers found a dead English soldier in a trench. In the final four lines, Aldington's aesthetic response reinstates this dead soldier's dignity: "More beautiful than one can tell, / More subtly coloured than a perfect Goya, / And more austere and lovely in repose / Than Angelo's hand could ever carve in stone."

"Bombardment" is a compellingly powerful description of the effects of lengthy bombardment on passive and helpless soldiers cowering in the ruined buildings of a village: lack of sleep, constant fear of annihilation, and nervous spasms. At the end of this ordeal the soldiers are able to emerge to see how above the pulverized earth "the white clouds moved in silent lines / Across the untroubled blue." The first and third stanzas begin with a portentous phrase that echoes the rhythm of biblical prose: "Four days the earth was rent and torn," and "The fifth day there came a hush."

Images of War ends with two poems concerning the disorientation of men just returned to civilian life in England. In the first, "Apathy," the poet addresses a silent monologue to the woman with whom he is walking. The returned ex-soldier's responses to the natural world are heightened and exaggerated. He doubts whether his companion can "interpret / These fragments of leaf-music" to the same degree of intensity as he can. The poet wonders if he can understand and combat his apathy: "While I struggle with myself, / Confront half-impulses, half-desires, / Grapple with lustreless definitions, / Grin at my inarticulate impotence / And so fall back on—apathy!" The poet indicates that he still possesses an appetite for life, and can still value beauty. His eyes focus on the subtle changes of color in the water flowing under a bridge, on water lilies, on insects and water plants. He is proud of his hypersensitive awareness of natural beauty. However, a jarring memory of the war irrupts into this idyllic scene; "And yet there's always something else—/ The way one corpse held its stiff yellow fingers / And pointed, pointed to the huge dark hole / Gouged between ear and jaw right to the skull." Without being aware of what he is doing, the poet utters a macabre laugh, apologizes to his companion, and explains it away as an unrepeatable story he heard yesterday. The final line, "Forgive me; I'll not laugh so suddenly again," offers a grim suggestion of the poet's future state of mind.

The next poem, "The Blood of the Young Men," is the work of a mind nearly at the end of its tether. It combines nightmarish visions of suffering and death with acerbic censure of heartless and insensitive civilians. It is full of repetitions, especially concerning blood. The words "blood" and "blood-stains" recur with hammering insistence in all eight of the poem's sections.

Images of War ends with "Epilogue" and a reference to Dante's *Inferno*. In this brief poem the poet likens himself and his fellow suffering soldiers to the victims in Dante's poem. The poet claims the hell they passed through was even "fiercer," "gloomier," and "more desperate" than Dante's, "And yet love kept us glad."

As Fred Crawford rightly says: "Aldington's war poetry offers a much wider range of immediate sensation and a more realistic perception of the war than do the verses of most of the trench poets."[90] Indeed, *Images of War* is one of the most coherent and comprehensive of all the collections of war poetry.

Proem

Out of this turmoil and passion,
This implacable contest,
This vast sea of effort,
I would gather something of repose,
Some intuition of the inalterable gods.

Each day I grow more restless,
See the austere shape elude me,
Gaze impotently upon a thousand miseries
And still am dumb.

Vicarious Atonement

This is an old and very cruel god. . . .

We will endure;
We will try not to wince
When he crushes and rends us.

64

If indeed it is for your sakes,
If we perish or moan in torture,
Or stagger under sordid burdens
That you may live—
Then we can endure.

If our wasted blood
Make bright the page
Of poets yet to be;
If this our tortured life
Save from destruction's nails
Gold words of a Greek long dead;
Then we can endure,
Then hope,
Then watch the sun rise
Without utter bitterness.

But, O thou old and very cruel god,
Take, if thou will, this bitter cup from us.

Leave-Taking

Will the world still live for you
When I am gone?

Will the straight garden poppy
Still spout blood from its green throat
Before your feet?
Will the five cleft petals of the campion
Still be rose-coloured,
Like five murdered senses, for you?

Will your trees still live,
Thrust metallic bosses of leafage
From the hillside in the summer light;
Will the leaves sway and grow darker,
Rustle, swirl in the gales;
Decay into gold and orange,
Crinkle and shrivel,

And fall silently at last
On to frosty grass?
Will there be sun for you;
The line of near hills
Cut as in thin blue steel
Against red haze?

Will there be silence?

Will not even the clean acrid sea
Turn stale upon your lips?

Will the world die for you
As it dies for me?

Bondage

I have been a spendthrift—
Dropping from lazy fingers
Quiet coloured hours,
Fluttering away from me
Like oak and beech leaves in October.

I have lived keenly and wastefully,
Like a bush or a sun insect—
Lived sensually and thoughtfully,
Loving the flesh and the beauty of this world—
Green ivy about ruined towers,
The outpouring of the grey sea,
And the ecstasy
Of a pale clear sky at sunset.

I have been prodigal of love
For cities and for lonely places;
I have tried not to hate mankind;
I have gathered sensations
Like ripe fruits in a rich orchard. . . .
All this is gone;
There are no leaves, no sea,
No shade of a rich orchard,

Only a sterile, dusty waste,
Empty and threatening.
I long vainly for solitude,
And the lapse of silent hours;
I am frantic to throw off
My heavy cloth and leather garments,
To set free my feet and body.
And I am so far from beauty
That a yellow daisy seems to clutch my heart
With eager searching petals,
And I am grateful even to humility
For the taste of pure clean bread.

Field Manoeuvres

Outpost Duty

The long autumn grass under my body
Soaks my clothes with its dew;
Where my knees press into the ground
I can feel the damp earth.

In my nostrils is the smell of the crushed grass,
Wet pine-cones and bark.

Through the great bronze pine trunks
Glitters a silver segment of road.
Interminable squadrons of silver and blue horses
Pace in long ranks the blank fields of heaven.

There is no sound;
The wind hisses gently through the pine needles;
The flutter of a finch's wing about my head
Is like distant thunder,
And the shrill cry of a mosquito
Sounds loud and close.

I am 'to fire at the enemy column
After it has passed'—
But my obsolete rifle, loaded with 'blank',

Lies untouched before me,
My spirit follows after the gliding clouds,
And my lips murmur of the mother of beauty
Standing breast-high, in golden broom
Among the blue pine-woods!

Dawn

The grim dawn lightens thin bleak clouds;
In the hills beyond the flooded meadows
Lies death-pale, death-still mist.
We trudge along wearily,
Heavy with lack of sleep,
Spiritless, yet with pretence of gaiety.

The sun brings crimson to the colourless sky;
Light shines from brass and steel;
We trudge on wearily—
Our unspoken prayer:
'God, end this black and aching anguish
Soon, with vivid crimson agonies of death,
End it in mist-pale sleep.'

The Lover

Though I have had friends
And a beautiful love
There is one lover I await above all.

She will not come to me
In the time of soft plum-blossoms
When the air is gay with birds singing
And the sky is a delicate caress;
She will come
From the midst of a vast clamour
With a mist of stars about her
And great beckoning plumes of smoke
Upon her leaping horses.

And she will bend suddenly and clasp me;
She will clutch me with fierce arms
And stab me with a kiss like a wound
That bleeds slowly.

But though she will hurt me at first
In her strong gladness
She will soon soothe me gently
And cast upon me an unbreakable sleep
Softly for ever.

A Moment's Interlude

One night I wandered alone from my comrades' huts;
The grasshoppers chirped softly
In the warm misty evening;
Bracken fronds beckoned from the darkness
With exquisite frail green fingers;
The tree-gods muttered affectionately about me
And from the distance came the grumble of a kindly train.

I was so happy to be alone
So full of love for the great speechless earth,
That I could have laid my cheek in the grasses
And caressed with my lips the hard sinewy body
Of Earth, the cherishing mistress of bitter lovers.

Insouciance

In and out of the dreary trenches
Trudging cheerily under the stars
I make for myself little poems
Delicate as a flock of doves.

They fly away like white-winged doves.

On the March

Bright berries on the roadside,
Clear among your dusty leaves,
Red mottled berries,
You are beautiful
As the points of a girl's breasts;
You are as firm and fresh.

Beauty of the morning sun
Among the red berries
Of early September,
You tear at my breast,
Your light crushes me
With memory of freedom lost
And warm hours blotted out.

I will throw away rifle and leather belt,
Straps, khaki and heavy nailed boots,
And run naked across the dewy grass
Among the firm red berries!
I will be free
And sing of beauty and the women of Hellas,
Of rent seas and the peace of olive gardens,
Of these rough meadows,
Of the keen welcome smell of London mud!
I will be free. . . .

Party—HALT!

In the Trenches

1

Not that we are weary,
Not that we fear,
Not that we are lonely
Though never alone—
Not these, not these destroy us;

70

But that each rush and crash
Of mortar and shell,
Each cruel bitter shriek of bullet
That tears the wind like a blade,
Each wound on the breast of earth,
Of Demeter, our Mother,
Wound us also,
Sever and rend the fine fabric
Of the wings of our frail souls,
Scatter into dust the bright wings
Of Psyche!

2

Impotent,
How impotent is all this clamour,
This destruction and contest. . . .
Night after night comes the moon
Haughty and perfect;
Night after night the Pleiades sing
And Orion swings his belt across the sky.
Night after night the frost
Crumbles the hard earth.

Soon the spring will drop flowers
And patient creeping stalk and leaf
Along these barren lines
Where huge rats scuttle
And the hawk shrieks to the carrion crow.

Can you stay them with your noise?
Then kill winter with your cannon,
Hold back Orion with your bayonets
And crush the spring leaf with your armies!

Ananke[91]

In bitter sorrow and despair
I said unto my love:
'All the far meadows, the cool marsh
And scented uplands I have searched
For blossoms pleasant to the gods;
I have begged just ripened fruits
From all the pitying tree-nymphs,
Have gathered many honey-combs,
Poured wine,
Poured milk,
Poured all my words in vain—
For yet the implacable gods
Turn their untroubled faces
Austerely from me,
Yet the cold envious wind
Whispers that no man born
Tricks the wide-open eyes of Fate'.

And seeing the pallor of her cheek,
Her fear-tormented eyes and tremulous hands,
I turned aside
To check the desperate tears burning my eyes;
Then came to her again, smiling,
And kissed her lips,
Saying no word save this:
'Do not despair'.

But yet
I have not seen her since that day.

Misery

Sometimes in bitter mood I mock myself:
'Half ape, half ass, servant and slave,
Where are your dreams gone now,
Where your fierce pride?
Whither goes your youth?
And how will you dare touch again

Dear slender women with those disfigured hands?
Or bare your long-dishonoured body
To the contemptuous sun?
How live after this shame?'

And all my answer:
'So that hate poison not my days,
And I still love the earth,
Flowers and all loving things,
And my song still be keen and clear
I can endure.'

Living Sepulchres

One frosty night when the guns were still
I leaned against the trench
Making for myself *hokku*[92]
Of the moon and flowers and of the snow.

But the ghostly scurrying of huge rats
Swollen with feeding upon men's flesh
Filled me with shrinking dread.

Daughter of Zeus

Tuerons la lune [Marinetti]

No!
We will not slay the moon.
For she is the fairest of the daughters of Zeus,
Of the maidens of Olympus.

And though she be pale and yet more pale
Gazing upon dead men
And fierce disastrous strife,
Yet for us she is still a frail lily
Floating upon a calm pool—
Still a tall lady comforting our human despair.

Picket

Dusk and deep silence . . .

Three soldiers huddled on a bench
Over a red-hot brazier,
And a fourth who stands apart
Watching the cold rainy dawn.

Then the familiar sound of birds—
Clear cock-crow, caw of rooks,
Frail pipe of linnet, the 'ting! ting!' of chaffinches,
And over all the lark
Outpiercing even the robin . . .

Wearily the sentry moves
Muttering the one word: 'Peace'.

Trench Idyll

We sat together in the trench,
He on a lump of frozen earth
Blown in the night before,
I on an unexploded shell;
And smoked and talked, like exiles,
Of how pleasant London was,
Its women, restaurants, night clubs, theatres,
How at that very hour
The taxi-cabs were taking folk to dine. . . .
Then we sat silent for a while
As a machine-gun swept the parapet.

He said:
'I've been here on and off two years
And seen only one man killed'.
'That's odd.'

'The bullet hit him in the throat;
He fell in a heap on the fire-step,
And called out "My God! *dead!*" '

'Good Lord, how terrible!'

'Well, as to that, the nastiest job I've had
Was last year on this very front
Taking the discs at night from men
Who'd hung for six months on the wire
Just over there.
The worst of all was
They fell to pieces at a touch.
Thank God we couldn't see their faces;
They had gas helmets on . . . '

I shivered;
'It's rather cold here, sir, suppose we move?'

Time's Changes

Four years ago today in Italy
I gathered wild flowers for a girl—
Thick scented broom, wild sword-flowers,
The red anemones that line the ways
And the frail-throated freesia
Which lives beneath the orange boughs
And whose faint scent to me
Is love's own breath, its kiss. . . .

Today in sunless barren fields
I gather heads of shells,
Splinters of shrapnel, cartridges. . . .

What shall I gather
Four years from today?

A Village

1

Now if you saw my village
You'd not think it beautiful,
But flat and commonplace—
As I'd have called it half a year ago. . . .

2

But when you've pondered
Hour upon chilly hour in those damned trenches
You get at the significance of things,
Get to know, clearer than before,
What a tree means, what a pool,
Or a black wet field in sunlight.

You get to know,
In that shell-pierced silence,
Under the unmoved ironic stars,
How good love of the earth is.

So I go strolling,
Hands deep in pockets, head aslant,
And eyes screwed up against the light,
Just loving things
Like any other lunatic or lover.

3

For there's so much to love,
So much to see and understand,
So much naïveté, whimsicality,
Even in a dull village like this.

Pigeons and fowls upon a pointed haystack;
The red-tiled barns we sleep in;
The profile of the distant town
Misty against the leaden-silver sky;
Two ragged willows and a fallen elm

With an end of broken wall
Glimmering through evening mist—
All worthy Rembrandt's hand,
Rembrandt who loved homely things. . . .

Then there's the rain pool where we wash,
Skimming the film-ice with our tingling hands;
The elm-fringed dykes and solemn placid fields
Flat as a slate and blacker.
There's the church—
The poorest ever built, I think—
With all its painted plaster saints
Straight from the Rue St Sulpice,
Its dreadful painted windows,
And Renaissance 'St Jacques le Majeur'
Over the porch. . . .

4

Today the larks are up,
The willow boughs are red with sap,
The last ice melting on the dykes;
One side there stands a row of poplars,
Slender amazons, martial and tall,
And on the other
The sunlight makes the red-tiled roofs deep orange. . . .

5

And we have come from death,
From the long weary nights and days
Out in those frozen wire-fringed ditches;
And this is life again, rich life—
This poor drab village, lovely in our eyes
As the prince city of Tuscany
Or the crown of Asia, Damascus.

The Wine Cup

Life was to us an amphora of wine
Pressed from full grapes
Upon the warm slopes of the Cyclades—
Wine that brings light
Into the gloomiest eyes of man,
Wine, cooled and mingled for the eager lip.

We had but gazed upon the amphora,
Touching the figures painted on its flanks—
Achilles reining in his four great horses
Or Maenads dancing to a Faun's pipe.

We had but sipped the wine,
Watching its changing hue—
Deep purple in the shadowy amphora
But crimson where the light
Pierces the crystal cup.

And if we thought:
'True, the cup soon is emptied,
The amphora rings hollow
And our veins lack warmth and life'—
It did but give a gentle melancholy
Making our present joy more keen and clear.

But now
Cold terrible, unseen hands
Have dragged the cup from us.
We are distracted
As a poor goatherd of the Thracian hills
Robbed of his flock and sun-tanned wife
Hurrying in anguish to the unfriendly town
As we to death.

Machine Guns

Gold flashes in the dark,
And on the road
Each side, behind, in front of us,
Gold sparks
Where the fierce bullets strike the stones.

In a near shell-hole lies a wounded man,
The stretcher-bearers bending over him;
And at our feet
Cower shrinkingly against the ground
Dark shadowy forms of men.

Only we two stand upright;
All differences of life and character smoothed out
And nothing left
Save that one foolish tie of caste
That will not let us shrink.

Battlefield

The wind is piercing chill
And blows fine grains of snow
Over this shell-rent ground;
Every house in sight
Is smashed and desolate.

But in this fruitless land,
Thorny with wire
And foul with rotting clothes and sacks,
The crosses flourish—
Ci-gît, ci-gît, ci-gît . . .

'Ci-gît I soldat Allemand,

Priez pour lui.

Three Little Girls[93]

Marianne, Madeline, Alys,
Three little girls I used to see
Two months ago,
Three little girls with fathers killed
And mothers lost,
Three little girls with broken shoes
And hard sharp coughs,
Three little girls who sold us sweets
Too near the shells,
Three little girls with names of saints
And angels' eyes.
Three little girls, where are you now?
Marianne, Madeline, Alys.

A Ruined House

Those who lived here are gone
Or dead or desolate with grief;
Of all their life here nothing remains
Except their trampled, dirtied clothes
Among the dusty bricks,
Their marriage bed, rusty and bent,
Thrown down aside as useless;
And a broken toy left by their child. . . .

Soliloquy—1

No, I'm not afraid of death
(Not very much afraid, that is)
Either for others or myself;
Can watch them coming from the line
On the wheeled silent stretchers
And not shrink,
But munch my sandwich stoically
And make a joke, when 'it' has passed.

But—the way they wobble!—
God! that makes one sick.
Dead men should be so still, austere,
And beautiful,
Not wobbling carrion roped upon a cart . . .

Well, thank God for rum.

[*New Paths. . . . 1917–18*, London, 1918]

Soliloquy–2

I was wrong, quite wrong;
The dead men are not always carrion.
After the advance,
As we went through the shattered trenches
Which the enemy had left,
We found, lying upon the fire-step,
A dead English soldier,
His head bloodily bandaged
And his closed left hand touching the earth,

More beautiful than one can tell,
More subtly coloured than a perfect Goya,
And more austere and lovely in repose
Than Angelo's hand could ever carve in stone.

[*New Paths. . . . 1917–18*, London, 1918]

A Young Tree

There are so few trees here, so few young trees,
That Fate might have been merciful
And turned aside the shock of flame
That strewed your branches on the turned-up earth,
Ending the joy we had in your fresh leaves.

And every keen dear lad that's killed
Seems to cry out:
'We are so few, so very few,
Could not our fate have been more merciful?'

81

Reverie

It is very hot in the chalk trench
With its rusty iron pickets
And shell-smashed crumbling traverses,
Very hot and choking and full of evil smells
So that my head and eyes ache
And I am glad to crawl away
And lie in the little shed I call mine.
And because I want to be alone
They keep coming to me and asking:
'How many billets have we in such a trench?'
Or, 'Do you know the way to such a redoubt?'

But these things pass over, beyond and away from me,
The voices of the men fade into silence
For I am burned with a sweet madness,
Soothed also by the fire that burns me,
Exalted and made happy in misery
By love, by an unfaltering love.
If I could tell you of this love—
But I can tell only lovers,
Only irresponsible imprudent lovers
Who give and have given and will give
All for love's sake,
And just to kiss her hand, her frail hand.

I will not tell you how long it is
Since I kissed and touched her hand
And was happy looking at her,
Yet every day and every night
She seems to be with me, beside me,
And there is great love between us
Although we are so far apart.

And although the hot sun burns in the white trench
And the shells go shrilling overhead
And I am harassed by stupid questions,
I do not forget her,
I do not forget to build dreams of her
That are only less beautiful than she is.

For there are some who love God,
And some their country and some gain,
Some are happy to exact obedience
And some to obey for the sake of a cause—
But I am indifferent to all these things
Since it was for her sake only I was born
So that I should love her.

Perhaps I shall be killed and never see her again,
Perhaps it will be but a wreck of me that returns to her,
Perhaps I shall kiss her hand once more,
But I am quite happy about Fate,
For this is love's beauty
That it does not die with lovers
But lives on, like a flower born from a god's blood,
Long after the lovers are dead.

Reason has pleaded in my brain
And Despair has whispered in my heart
That we die and vanish utterly;
I have seen dead men lying on the earth
Or carried slowly in stretchers,
And the chilled blood leaped in my heart
Saying: 'This is the end, there is no escape'.

But for love's sake I brush all this away
For, since I do not know why love is
Nor whence it comes, nor for what end,
It may very well be that I am wrong about death,
And that among the dead also there are lovers.

Would that we were dead, we two,
Dead centuries upon centuries,
Forgotten, even our race and tongue forgotten,
Would that we had been dead so long
That no memory of this fret of life
Could ever trouble us.

We would be together, always together
Always in a land of many flowers,
And bright sunlight and cool shade;

We should not even need to kiss
Or join our hands;
It would be enough to be together.

She would stoop and gather a flower,
A pale, sweet-scented, fragile flower
(A flower whose name I will not tell,
The symbol of all love to us).

And I would watch her smile
And see the fair flowers of her breast
As the soft-coloured garment opened from her throat.

I would not speak, I would not speak one word
Though many ages of the world's time passed—
She would be bending by the flower's face
And I would stand beside and look and love.

Not far away as I now write
The guns are beating madly upon the still air
With sudden rapid blows of sound,
And men die with the quiet sun above them
And horror and pain and noise upon earth.

Tomorrow, maybe, I shall be one of them,
One in a vast field of dead men,
Unburied, or buried hastily, callously.
But for ever and for ever
In the fair land I have built up
From the dreams of my love,
We two are together, she bending by the pale flower
And I beside her:
We two together in a land of quiet
Inviolable behind the walls of death.

[First published in *Reverie: A Little Book of Poems for H.D.* Cleveland: Clerk's Press, 1917]

April Lieder

When I rose up this morning
In a ruined town of France,
I heard the sparrows twitter
In gardens bare and grey
And watched the sunbeams dance.

O glad young April day!

When I lie down this evening
In a damp cellar of France
I'll hear the big guns booming
By bare and blasted lanes,
And watch the shrapnel dance.

O wild sad April rains!

Barrage

Thunder,
The gallop of innumerable Valkyrie impetuous for battle,
The beating of vast eagle wings above Prometheus,
The contest of tall barbaric gods smitten by the hammer
   of Thor,
Pursuit! Pursuit! Pursuit!
The huge black dogs of hell
Leaping full-mouthed in murderous pursuit!

An Earth Goddess

You are not the august Mother
Nor even one of her comely daughters,
But you gave shelter to men,
Hid birds and little beasts within your hands
And twined flowers in your hair.

Sister, you have been sick of a long fever,
You have been torn with throes
Fiercer than childbirth and yet barren;
You are plague-marked;
There are now no flowers in your hair.

I have seen your anguish, O Sister,
I have seen your wounds.
But now there is come upon you peace,
A peace unbroken, profound,
Such as came upon the mother of King Eteocles
When both her sons were dead.
For in your agony, Sister,
When men bruised and ravished you,
You remembered the wide kindness of our Mother
And gave shelter to each of them that rent you,
Shielded them from death with your delicate body
And received their clotted corpses into your once pure breast.

And now since you endured,
Since for all your wrong and bitter pain
There came no hatred upon you
But only pity and anguish
Such as the mother of King Eteocles felt
Gazing upon her two angry sons—
Because of this, your peace is wonderful.

Underfoot are a few scant grasses
Amid rusty ruin;
Overhead the last of your larks
Cries shrilly before the broken clouds;
But for your sake, O my Sister,
O daughter of our great Earth-Mother,
Because of your old pain
And long-suffering and sweetness,
Because of the new peace
Which lies so deeply upon you,
The chains of my bitterness are broken,
The weight of my despair leaves me.

Bombardment

Four days the earth was rent and torn
By bursting steel,
The houses fell about us;
Three nights we dared not sleep,
Sweating, and listening for the imminent crash
Which meant our death.

The fourth night every man,
Nerve-tortured, racked to exhaustion,
Slept, muttering and twitching,
While the shells crashed overhead.

The fifth day there came a hush;
We left our holes
And looked above the wreckage of the earth
To where the white clouds moved in silent lines
Across the untroubled blue.

Epitaph

1

H.S.R. Killed April 1917

You are dead—
You, the kindly, the courteous,
You whom we loved,
You who harmed no man
Yet were brave to death
And died that other men might live.

Far purer, braver lips than mine should praise you,
Far nobler hands than mine record your loss,
Yet since your courteous high valour scorned no man,
I, who but loved you from the ranks, can greet you,
Salute your grave and murmur: 'Brother,
Hail and Farewell'.

Epitaph

2

E.T. Killed May 1917

You too are dead,
The coarse and ignorant,
Carping against all that was too high
For your poor spirit to grasp,
Cruel and evil-tongued—
Yet you died without a moan or whimper.

Oh, not I, not I should dare to judge you!
But rather leave with tears your grave
Where the sweet grass will cover all your faults
And all your courage too.

Brother, hail and farewell.

Concert

These antique prostitutions—
I deplore my own vague cynicism,
Undressing with indifferent eyes each girl,
Seeing them naked on that paltry stage
Stared at by half a thousand lustful eyes.

These antique prostitutions—
Am I dead? Withered? Grown old?
That not the least flush of desire
Tinges my unmoved flesh,
And that instead of women's living bodies
I see dead men—you understand?—dead men
With sullen, dark red gashes
Luminous in a foul trench?

These antique prostitutions.

Taintignies

Belgium

This land is tedious as a worn-out whore;
Faded and shabby
As her once bright face
Grown tarnished with disease,
Loathsome as her grin which shows
The black cubes of the missing teeth;
The very sky is drab and sear
As her lifeless hair,
The earth itself rotten and foul
As her dishonoured flesh.

Terror

1

Those of the earth envy us,
Envy our beauty and frail strength,
Those of the wind and the moon
Envy our pain.

2

For as doe that has never borne child
We were swift to fly from terror;
And as fragile edged steel
We turned, we pierced, we endured.

3

We have known terror;
The terror of the wind and silent shadows,
The terror of great heights,
The terror of the worm,
The terror of thunder and fire,

The terror of water and slime,
The terror of horror and fear,
The terror of desire and pain—
The terror of apathy.

4

As a beast, as an arrow of pine,
Terror cleft us,
Tore us in envy away,
So that for month upon month
Pain wore us, hope left us, despair clutched us,
For they of the earth envied us,
Envied our beauty and strength.

5

Yet because, though we faltered and wept,
We held fast, clung close to our love,
Scorned hate even as they scorned us,
Some god has lightened our lives
Given back the cool mouth of song,
The mouth crushed like a flower.

6

We have suffered, we have bled,
And those of the wind and the moon
Envy our pain, the pain of the terror,
The delight no terror could slay.

Defeat

Though our hearts were mad and strong
With love for you,
Though we fought for you,
Though our remnant struggled
And not one was false,
We are beaten.

Beauty, for your sake we are lost,
For you we are crushed,
Scorn and bitterness are cast at us,
And fools who hate you
Are preferred to us.

Treacherous wonderful lady,
You have betrayed us—
Yet, hurt and overwhelmed and in despair
We can but turn to you again
And sing our love for you.

White goddess of beauty,
Take these roses—
It is our blood that colours them;
Take these lilies—
White as our intense hearts;
Take these wind-flowers—
Frail as our strength spent in your service;
Take these hyacinths—
Graven with the sigh of our lost days;
Take these narcissus blooms
Lovely as your naked breasts.

White goddess of beauty,
Though the stars rose against you
And the steeds of the day
Were arrayed against you,
Though the might of the sea
And the menace of night
Were against you,
We would be with you
And worship you.

Ah, goddess! Lovely, implacable,
What wine shall we bring,
What cup for your lips?
Blood, blood of our hearts for a drink,
Our lives for a cup.

White grape and red grape and pale
Dim scarlet of wearied mouths,

Flowers and the music of trees,
Hills golden with sun
And the sea, still and blue and divine—
These are yours
But not ours.

We are scorned for your sake,
We are broken,
Ah, goddess! You turn from our pain!

And once we begged of you death,
Death quiet and smiling,
Death cold as the wind of the sea.

Now, love has lighted our hearts,
Now, though we are beaten and crushed,
Grant us life.

Grant us life to suffer for you,
To feed your delicate lips,
With the strength of our blood,
To crown you with flowers of our pain
And hail you with cries of our woe,
Yet sweet and divine.

Grant us life!
If we die there is none upon earth
To feed the fierce pride of your heart;
There is none so fine and so keen,
There is none to sing at your feast.

Grant us life,
And gold lyre and box-wood pipe
Shall sound from hill-top and shore,
From the depth of the city street,
From under the horror of battle,
Faint as we faint in despair,
Yet clear in your praise.

We dream of white crags,
Skies changing and swift,

Of rain upon earth,
Of flowers soft as your fingers
And bright as your garments of love.

We have none of these things;
Only strife and despair and pain,
Lands hideous and days disfigured,
A grey sea and a muddy shore.
But for you we forget all this,
We forget our defeat,
All, all for your sake.

Doubt

1

Can we, by any strength of ours
Thrust back this hostile world
That tears us from ourselves,
As a child from the womb,
A weak lover from light breasts?

Is there any hope?
Can we believe
That not in wild perversity,
In blinding cruelty,
Has flesh torn flesh,
Has soul been torn from soul?

Must we despair?
Throw back upon the gods this taunt
That even their loveliest is at best
Some ineffectual lie?

2

Sand in the gale whirls up,
Pricks and stifles our flesh,
Blinds and deafens our sense

So that we cannot hear
The crumbling downfall of the waves
Nor see the limpid sunlight any more.

But could we thrust from us
This threat, this misery,
Borrow the mountain's strength
As now its loneliness,
Hurl back this menace on itself,
Crush bronze with bronze—

Why, it would be as if some tall slim god
Unburdened of his age-long apathy,
Took in his hand the thin horn of the moon
And set it to his lips
And blew sharp wild shrill notes
Such as our hearts, our lonely hearts,
Have yearned for in the dumb bleak silences.

3

Ah! Weak as wax against their bronze are we,
Ah! Faint as reed-pipes by the water's roar,
And driven as land-birds by the vast sea wind.

Resentment

Why should you try to crush me?
Am I so Christ-like?

You beat against me,
Immense waves, filthy with refuse.
I am the last upright of a smashed breakwater
But you shall not crush me
Though you bury me in foaming slime
And hiss your hatred about me.

You break over me, cover me;
I shudder at the contact;

Yet I pierce through you
And stand up, torn, dripping, shaken,
But whole and fierce.

Disdain

Have the gods then left us in our need
Like base and common men?
Were even the sweet grey eyes
Of Artemis a lie,
The speech of Hermes but a trick,
The glory of Apollonian hair deceit?

Desolate we move across a desolate land,
The high gates closed,
No answer to our prayer;
Naught left save our integrity,
No murmur against Fate
Save that we are juster than the unjust gods,
More pitiful than they.

Apathy

Come down the road and do not speak.
You cannot know how strange it is
To walk again upon a grey firm road again,
To feel the noiseless waves of air break on one's flesh.

You do not speak, you do not look at me;
Just walk in silence on the grey firm road
Guessing my mood by instinct, not by thought—
For there is no weapon of tongue or glance
So keen that it can stir my apathy,
Can stab that bitterness to hope,
Can pierce that humour to despair.

Silence fits the mood then—silence and you.

The trees beside the road—can you interpret
These fragments of leaf-music,
Here a phrase, and here a sort of melody
That dies to silence or is broken
By a full rustling that is discord?
Can you interpret such a simple thing?

Can I interpret this blank apathy,
This humorous bitterness?
Lean on the bridge now—do not speak—
And watch the coloured water slipping past,
While I struggle with myself,
Confront half-impulses, half-desires,
Grapple with lustreless definitions,
Grin at my inarticulate impotence
And so fall back on—apathy!

The bridge has three curved spans,
Is made of weathered stones,
And rests upon two diamond-pointed piers—
Is picturesque.
(I have not lost all touch and taste for life,
See beauty just as keenly, relish things.)
The water here is black and specked with white;
Under that tree the shallows grow to brown,
Light amber where the sunlight struggles through—
And yet what colour is it if you watch the reeds
Or if you only see the trees' reflection?

Flat on the surface rest the lily leaves
(Some curled up inwards, though, like boats)
And yellow heads thrust up on fine green throats.
Two—three—a dozen—watch now—demoiselle flies
Flicker and flutter and dip and rest
Their beryl-green or blue, dark Prussian blue, frail wings
On spits and threads of water-plant.
Notice all carefully, be precise, welcome the world.
Do I miss these things? Overlook beauty?
Not even the shadow of a bird
Passing across that white reflected cloud.

And yet there's always something else—
The way one corpse held its stiff yellow fingers
And pointed, pointed to the huge dark hole
Gouged between ear and jaw right to the skull.

Did I startle you? What was the matter?
Just a joke they told me yesterday,
Really, really, not for ladies' ears.
Forgive me; I'll not laugh so suddenly again.

The Blood of the Young Men

1

Give us back the close veil of the senses,
Let us not see, ah, hide from us
The red blood splashed upon the walls,
The good red blood, the young, the lovely blood
Trampled unseeingly by passing feet,
Feet of the old men, feet of the cold cruel women,
Feet of the careless children, endlessly passing. . . .

2

Day has become an agony, night alone now,
That leisurely shadow, hides the blood-stains,
The horrible stains and clots of day-time.

3

All the garments of all the people,
All the wheels of all the traffic,
All the cold indifferent faces,
All the fronts of the houses,
All the stones of the street—
Ghastly! Horribly smeared with blood-stains.

4

The horror of it!
When a woman holds out a white hand
Suddenly to know it drips black putrid blood;
When an old man sits, serene and healthy,
In clean white linen, with clean white hair,
Suddenly to know the linen foully spotted,
To see white hair streaked with dripping blood.

5

O these pools and ponds of blood,
Slowly dripped in, slowly brimming lakes,
Blood of the young men, blood of their bodies,
Squeezed and crushed out to purple the garments of Dives,
Poured out to colour the lips of Magdalen,
Magdalen who loves not, whose sins are loveless.
O this steady drain of the weary bodies,
This beating of hearts growing dimmer and dimmer,
This bitter indifference of the old men,
This exquisite indifference of women.

6

Old men, you will grow stronger and healthier
With broad red cheeks and clear hard eyes—
Are not your meat and drink the choicest?
Blood of the young, dear flesh of the young men?

7

Ah, you women, cruel exquisite women,
What a love-fountain is poured out for you,
What coloured streams for your pleasure!
Go your ways, pass on, forget them;
Give your lips and breasts to the old men,
The kindly, impetuous, glowing, old men!
They who love you indeed, indeed, dears,
Not as we do, drained of our blood, with weeping,
Sell yourselves, oh, give yourselves to the cripples,

Give yourselves to the weak, the poor forgotten,
Give yourselves to those who escape the torture
And buy their blood from the pools with weight of gold.

Give yourselves to them, pass on, forget us;
We, any few that are left, a remnant,
Sit alone together in cold and darkness,
Dare not face the light for fear we discover
The dread woe, the agony in our faces,
Sit alone without sound in bitter dreaming
Of our friends, our dear brothers, the young men,
Who were mangled and abolished, squeezed dry of blood,
Emptied and cast aside that the lakes might widen,
That the lips of the women might be sweet to the old men.

8

Go your ways, you women, pass and forget us,
We are sick of blood, of the taste and sight of it;
Go now to those who bleed not and to the old men,
They will give you beautiful love in answer!
But we, we are alone, we are desolate,
Thinning the blood of our brothers with weeping,
Crying for our brothers, the men we fought with,
Crying out, mourning them, alone with our dead ones;
Praying that our eyes may be blinded
Lest we go mad in a world of scarlet,
Dropping, oozing from the veins of our brothers.

Epilogue

Che son contenti nel fuoco

We are of those that Dante saw
Glad, for love's sake, among the flames of hell,
Outdaring with a kiss all-powerful wrath;
For we have passed athwart a fiercer hell,
Through gloomier, more desperate circles
Than ever Dante dreamed:
And yet love kept us glad.

Notes

88. Friedman, 1990, 138.
89. Smith, 1977, 69.
90. Crawford, 1988, 91.
91. Greek for "necessity."
92. Originally *hokku* was the first half line of a linked series of *haiku*. The *haiku* is a three-line poem of five, seven, and five syllables respectively. This strict Japanese form produces allusively imagistic verse.
93. In a letter of 22 January 1917 Aldington wrote to F. S. Flint: "There are also the graves of two little girls, killed by the same German shell. I often go and stand by them and think many things." Quoted in Gates, 1992, 24.

Part II
Additional Poems

The poems in this section are drawn from various sources. Four of them, "Any Woman to Any Soldier," "Mr. Klamp Addresses his Soul," "War is an Anachronism," and the longer version of "Happiness" remained unpublished until Norman Gates included them in his *The Poetry of Richard Aldington*. Of the remainder, some were published in magazines (*The Egoist, Coterie, Poetry: A Magazine of Verse,* and *The Living Age*), some in various collections of Aldington's poems (*Images of Desire, War and Love, Exile, Collected Poems, The Eaten Heart,* and *The Poems of Richard Aldington*), and two originally appeared in novels (*Death of a Hero* and *All Men are Enemies*).

The passionate eroticism of "Any Woman to Any Soldier" is expressed from the woman's point of view. The war for her is conveyed by the abstract generalization "hell." The poem is noteworthy for its strict adherence to meter (except for one octosyllabic line) and to an AB rhyme scheme. Such rigorous formal concerns are rare in Aldington's verse.

"Deaths of Common Men" begins by interweaving three themes: an idealized pastoral; the corrupting, negative influence of urban existence; and the grim reality of death and decay on the battlefield. After the sumptuous vision of the first three lines the poet indicates his purpose: to tell of the normality of death. City-dwellers have a distorted fear of death. In the third and fourth stanzas the poet contrasts their hysterical attitude with the stark reality of the deaths of soldiers that he has witnessed. The last four lines of the fourth stanza bring us back to the idyllic scene of the poem's beginning, the vine harvest, accompanied by warmth, wine, love, and laughter. The poet remains alive to savor this experience while his comrades have fallen in war. In the remaining four stanzas the poet earnestly urges his readers to grasp the earth in their hands, to realize that this earth contains the remains of all former living creatures, to feel at one with the earth. Twice he seeks to persuade ordinary folk not to feel inferior to "subtle men." The poet offers the reassurance that he is accustomed to looking at the dead, and says that after giving them "a last keen look, / Affectionate, valedictory," it is perfectly natural to bury them and to return to living one's life, "serious, but tranquil and cheerful." The poem ends with an expression of the view that human bodies are part of the earth that is enriched by our dying. We may infer that this enrichment is not only physical but intellectual and spiritual as well.

"Reserve" and the three poems that follow come from *Images of Desire*. These poems convey a deeply felt eroticism that is always sensual, and one that veers between wild passion and gentle tenderness. In "Before Parting" and "Daybreak" the poet's highly charged erotic memories have to compete with the harsh realities of trench warfare. "Daybreak" in particular contains some intensely violent moments as the poet seeks a form of death from his beloved: "take my life breath," "break / My body," "use my very / blood to slake / Your parching, sudden thirst of lust," "thrust your white teeth in my flesh," "slay me with your lips," and "kill my body's / strength and spirit's will." The effects the poet solicits bear an alarming resemblance to what might happen to his body when he returns to face the bullets and shells. "Reserve" is the shortest of all Aldington's war poems. After the opening three lines, which indicate the poet and his lover waking up in bed together, the poet reveals why he feels unable to respond to her, in spite of being "thrilled by your dark gold flesh." After this hint at voluptuous pleasure the fourth and final line comes as an abrupt shock: "I think of how the dead, my dead, once lay." "Meditation" finds the poet in far more contemplative mood, with the opportunity to indulge in anxious reflection. This poem, like "Reserve," contains an Aldington shock effect. After the first three lines that deftly sketch a wintry scene the moon is presented by means of a macabre image: "yellow and blotched, / Like the face of a six days' corpse," it "stares hideously over the barren wood." The poet looks forward to returning home to his beloved, to the charms of England and foreign cities, and to books. But now that he has time to dwell on such matters he cannot help having nagging doubts about her fidelity. He wonders if someone else is enjoying what he once enjoyed. Perhaps "her red mouth stabs him to passion / As it stabbed me." He then worries about being unable to resume his former life at all. He might feel alienated from "café-chatterers" with their "narrow shoulders." Further, he might prove to be "too sick at heart with overmuch slaughter / To dream quietly over books. / Too impatient of lies to cajole / Even my scanty pittance from the money-vultures." The poem ends on a very down-beat note, as the poet, pessimistic and resigned, wonders if the present moment might not, after all, be the happiest for him, "Remembering harsh years past, / Plotting gold years to come, / Trusting so blithely in a woman's faith."

The two poems entitled "Happiness" are alternative versions, with the shorter one almost certainly a later condensed form of the earlier longer one. The longer poem is more discursive, and Aldington seems to have jettisoned the first sixteen lines in order to tackle the source of his happiness in a tighter and more immediate way in the short version. The fact that the short version was published while the long version remained unpublished suggests that Aldington correctly judged the long poem to be less satisfactory, and that he used it as a draft, as source material for the short version. He was clearly keen to retain the effective image of the mist lying "like cream in a rough brown bowl." The economy and clarity of the last stanza in the short version is much to be preferred to the rather diffuse expression of the long version.

In "Eumenides" (from *Exile and Other Poems*, 1923) Aldington meditates on the issues of mortality, happiness, memory, and survival, and the effects that these thoughts have on him. In the first five stanzas he tells us it is at night that he thinks of what being alive means for him: "I have lived with, fed upon death / As happier generations feed upon life." The fourth stanza is a long litany of restorative pastoral in the rural retreat he has created for himself. Here he has found consolation, not only in nature, but also in books, friends, and work. Night, however, brings horrific visions of the trenches that prevent sleep. The sixth and seventh stanzas list these nightmare sights, starting with four generalities, places such as a "horrible night in Hart's Crater," the "damp cellars of Maroc," the "frozen ghostly streets of Vermelles," and one event, a "night-long gas bombardment." There follows a rapid succession of specific moments and occurrences: "That boot I kicked / (It had a mouldy foot in it)," and "The night K's head was smashed / Like a rotten pear by a mortar." At the beginning of the seventh stanza the poet refers to these "fearful memories of despair and misery" as "Eumenides," that is, avenging Furies. The sequence of memories accelerates in a swift succession of staccato impressions: "Tortured flesh, caked blood, endurance, / Men, men and the roar of shells, / The hissing lights, red, green, yellow, / The clammy mud, the tortuous wire, / The slippery boards." In stanza eight he is anxious to stress that his continued postwar torment is in no way unique, that he is not to be considered a special case abjectly pleading for pity and understanding: "It is all so stale, / It has been said a thousand times; / Millions have seen it, been it, as I; / Millions may be haunted by these spirits / As I am haunted." In the final stanza he explains that it is not for the dead that he agonizes, "They are quiet; / They can have no complaint," but for his "own murdered self—/ A self which had its passion for beauty, / Some moment's touch with immortality." This is what the Eumenides, these constantly recurring remembered images, represent: "It is myself that is the Eumenides." They are persistently seeking atonement for "the wrong that has been done me." The poem ends with the anguished question, "Tell me, what answer shall I give my murdered self?" Adrian Barlow has pointed out that among all the poets who treated the state of Britain before and during the war, as well as in the twenties Aldington is unique in doing so from his position of direct personal involvement in the war. His poetry of this period treats the "afterlife of the war and examines all the themes that ultimately are to coalesce into *Death of a Hero.*" His poetry deals with the shock of survival in the aftermath. This, ironically, enables us to understand how Aldington came to write a war novel in which the hero chose death.[94]

Indeed, "Eumenides," coming as it does after *Images of War*, and before the later long poems and *Death of a Hero*, must be seen as a key transitional work in the context of the development of Aldington's war-influenced writing.

"In the Palace Garden" voices one of Aldington's postwar problems, the dilemma of how to reconcile his postwar sense of well-being with a feeling of guilt at having survived when so many men had been killed. The simple pleasures of a walk in a park in the company of his beloved are initially sufficient to create a happy frame of mind. The thought that he is alive is at first adequate to supplement this mood: "It was enough not to be dead." This reflection, however, is not allowed to rest there. The idea of death does not remain an abstract concept, but surfaces in the form of a nightmarish memory of rotten flesh, "a black spongy mass of decay / Half-buried on the edge of a trench." The poet then starts wondering why the effect of these surrounding ele-

106

ments, which should be conducive to unalloyed happiness, begins to evaporate. The answer he gives himself comes in the final three lines: "This happiness is not yours; / It is stolen from other men. / Coward! You have shirked your fate." This is a further example of the ways in which Aldington's personal Eumenides return to haunt him.

"The Faun Complains" contrasts the idyllic natural world of Greek mythology, inhabited by fauns, dryads, and hamadryads, with the squalor, machinery and cruelty of war: "They give me aeroplanes / Instead of birds and moths; / Instead of sunny fields / They give me mud-holes." In the final two lines the mockery of "Odd, loud-voiced, fearsome men" is indicative of how aware Aldington was that the sensitive, creative, and artistic side of his personality was being warped, eroded and destroyed by the war machine.

In the later "In Memory of Wilfred Owen" Aldington's present euphoria continues to be disturbed by memories of the dead. But now, although recollections of the past are still acute, his spirit is less anguished and tormented. A mood of serenity has replaced the former distress. Aldington is addressing all the war dead rather than one individual. Nevertheless, there is one echo of Wilfred Owen present. Aldington's "When the hired buglers call unheeded to you" recalls Owen's "And bugles calling for them from sad shires" in "Anthem for Doomed Youth."

"By the King's Most Excellent Majesty: A Proclamation" can be regarded as Aldington's most modernist poem. In this collage-poem he epitomizes each year by quoting recognizable fragments from popular ditties of the war years. The mood changes from one of enthusiastic and jingoistic urging by civilians for men to enlist in the early months of the war to one of bleakly cynical resignation and black humor from the surviving men by the end of the war. The satirical effect is all the more powerful given that Aldington refrains from inserting his own words and from commenting on or reinforcing the message he is constructing out of this sequence of snippets.

Any Woman to Any Soldier

What is there left to say
    This side of hell,
What word to speak or pray
    Except "farewell"?

But, ere that bitterest sigh
    Pierces my brain,
Lift your bowed head on high,
    Kiss me again.

Lift up once more your head
    And let me taste
The last of many kisses shed
    On lips and breasts.

Kiss my writhed lips again
    This side of hell,
Kiss dumb the sob of pain
    And then—farewell.

2 February 1918

[Gates, 1974, 173.]

Deaths of Common Men

Now, while the sun is hot
And they gather the grape harvest,
And the leaves are gold, and life splendid,
Let me speak once more of the end, the parting—
How simple it is, how natural.

People in cities, perturbed, neurasthenic,
Rushing like futile hogs helter-skelter,
Living as if they would live for ever,
Dread death, shrink and shiver and mumble,
Start at the spectre, evade, palaver,
Till shoved ignominiously
Into the greasy grave.

More of my friends now are dead than living.
I have seen the strong body crumble and wither,
Give at the knees, stumble, crash in the mud,
Groan a little, lie still;
I have seen the good flesh cut, the white bone shattered,
Seen the red face turn like a yellow leaf,
The firm mouth wobble;
Watched it all, taken it in.

I have slept side by side with men
Who are now green corpses
Or bundles of dirty bones.
All of them, dozens, gone, and I only
Left above ground in the hot sun,
Tasting wine, wooing lips, laughing,
Watching the harvest, joking, sweating,
Alive.

Take earth in your hands, common earth,
Moist crumbly loam, dark, odorous—
This is the bodies of our forefathers,
Of long-ago mothers, beasts, insects;
See that you love the common earth,
Press it close in your hands
And murmur: "This is my body."

We are made of the infinite dead,
And, dead, we make the infinite living.
Have no fear of the subtle man,
The man of affected speech and brains;
You and I will make just as good corpses,
Our clay is sweeter.

Have no fear, I say, death is nothing;
I see dead men every week,
Give them a last keen look,
Affectionate, valedictory,
Then cover the face
And turn again to my life,
Serious, but tranquil and cheerful.

Again I say to you, simple folk,
Who, like me, are afraid of the great
And ill at ease with subtle men,
Have no fear;
We are—not the salt—
But the earth of the earth, earth itself,
And we die that life may be richer.

September 1918

[*The Egoist,* Vol. 5, No. 10, November–December 1918.
Gates, 1974, 264–65.]

Minor Exasperations

II Valhalla

The war-worn heroes take their rest
In the mess ante-room . . .

Some sprawl asleep by the stove,
Some play bridge on green tables,
Some read novels,
Mournfully peering through smoky air.

Thus, O Athene, do the high heroes,
Even as Odysseus and the noble Menelaus,
Rest from the toils of war.

Newhaven, 1918

III My Colonel

My colonel has several dabs of bright colour
Over his left top pocket;
He walks with harassed dignity;
His gaze of intelligence is deceptive—
There is nothing in his head
But a précis of King's Regs.,
Crime sheets and military handbooks.

Every day he talks seriously to poor fools
Who have stayed out too late at night
Or lost a rifle or forgotten to shave;
Nearly every day he condemns to prison
Some weak-minded son of Cain
For an absurd triviality.

I have never spoken unofficially to my colonel
But I suspect he is even more imbecile than I have painted him.

Newhaven, 1919

IV Breaking Point

Have I still three friends in the world
Untainted by moral cowardice,
By respect for institutions?

I will dance a solemn war dance,
Crouching down, beating my hands,
Solemnly stamping my feet;
I will dance on the grave of prosperity.
I lust for the scalp of smug security,
To rattle the bones of the bourgeois.

I will make mock of brass hats and brass buttons.
At a serious ceremonial moment
When the hero of a hundred newspapers
(The general who never saw the line)
Is inspecting a motionless brigade,
I will pierce the shocked air
With a laugh of preposterous ribaldry.

I will sneer at this silly war
(I have suffered, I can do as I please),
I will sneer at its bastard pomp,
Expose its flatulent hypocrisy.

O, I could charm the high gods
With a more than Aristophanic levity,

Deploy before their histrionic cachinnations
The biggest fraud in history;
O, I could play hell with this epoch
Had I still three friends in the world
Untainted by moral cowardice,
By respect for institutions.

Newhaven, 1918

[*Coterie,* No. 2, September 1919. Gates, 1974, 268–70.]

Mr. Klamp Addresses His Soul

Well, you got through. That's that. . . .

What next? Some tedious months
In a rain-logged Belgian village,
Then out you go—a hundred quid
To pay for three years of your life . . .

And after that?
Do you return to the old vomit,
The "literary life"—
Eunuchs of either sex discoursing
Over weak tea and sugary buns?
Ten hours a day of work
For some abuse and a hall porter's pay?
Culture on fifty bob a week? . . .

Well, what? Trade? You'd fail,
You know you'd fail.
A clerk? Hell, why not office boy?
What then? The Colonies?
You'd sooner die and add to Bethnal Green
One other inconspicuous stone? . . .

Cheer up! You're "one of England's heroes" . . .
There, don't be sick. Keep still,
Say what you do want . . .
Silent? I'll answer.
You want something worth while,

Something without the smirch of humbug,
Something a man who's looked on love and death
Can reverence, can die for if need be.
That's what you seek? . . .

Good friend, it were better for you
To lie at Ypres with the million dead
Than take such ancient homespun trash
To London, that great city. . . .

Take my advice,
Lie, humbug, scuffle with the rest,
Scratch for your pelf in the gutter,
Follow the Preacher that was king in Israel
And eat and drink and buy you women slaves
For all is vanity. . . .
No good?
Well, go and help the poor . . .

You're tired of vermin?
Well, I merely try
To find an issue for you.
If you spent your life, now,
In educating England's youth;
Educing from its urchins, shall we say,
Love of Greek verse? . . .

No?
Go in for politics,
You have a sort of supple back
And a gift of eloquent wind;
You might achieve—who knows?—
A half assistant-under-ushership . . .

Still restive?
Then turn Bolshevik
And wreck the world you can't possess
And lose the beauty you have never had . . .

Not even that?
Then go to hell, my soul,
And leave me to my piddling pursuits.

[Gates, 1974, 197–99.]

Reserve

Though you desire me I will still feign sleep
And check my eyes from opening to the day,
For as I lie, thrilled by your gold-dark flesh,
I think of how the dead, my dead, once lay.

[*Images of Desire*, 1919]

Before Parting

Love, though the whole earth rock
With the shattering roar of the guns' booming,
Though in that horror of din and flame and murder
All men's blood grows faint and their limbs as water,
Though I return once more to the battle,
Though perhaps I be lost to you for ever—
Give me, O love, your love for this last brief season,
Be mine indeed as I am yours.

Tonight there shall be no tears, no wearing sorrow,
No drawn-out agony of hope, no cold despairing,
Only we two together in a sudden glory
Of infinite delight and sharp sweet yearning,
Shutting out for a space the world's harsh horror.

Kiss my lips with your mouth that is wet with wine,
Wine that is only less keen than your lips are;
Slip from under your fragile garments as a white rose
Slips from under her leaves to the naked sunlight;
Give to my eyes your straight young body,
The limbs that embrace me, the breasts that caress me,
Whisper to me the sudden words of yearning,
The broken words that speak an infinite yearning
That delight would last for ever, love never to be ended. . . .

Give me this and I care not if death come after,
For tonight there shall be no tears, no wearing sorrow,
Only our kisses and whispers and stabbing heart-beats.

[*Images of Desire*, 1919]

114

Daybreak

The naked pale limbs of the dawn lie sheathed
    in dove-white folds of lawn
But from one scarlet breast I see the cloudy
    cover slowly drawn.

Not all the blood of all our dead, the bright,
    gay blood so gaily shed,
Shines with so clear a glow as gleams your breast-
    flower from our candid bed.

Ah, bend above me, dear, and take my life breath
    with your lips and break
My body up as wheaten bread, and use my very
    blood to slake

Your parching sudden thirst of lust. Be cruel,
    love, be fierce and thrust
Your white teeth in my flesh and taste how
    honey-sweet is amorous dust.

Ah! slay me with your lips, ah! kill my body's
    strength and spirit's will
So that at dawn I need not go but lie between
    your breast-flowers still.

[Images of Desire, 1919]

Meditation

Outside the young frost crisps the grass
And bends the narrow willow boughs
And flecks the dyke with little spears of ice;
The huge moon, yellow and blotched,
Like the face of a six days' corpse,
Stares hideously over the barren wood.

In the silence, the deep pool-like silence,
Untroubled by crash of guns or tramp of men,

115

I sit alone in a small Belgian house
And stare against the moon and feel
Silence like a slow wave of the outer sea
Drive over and through me,
Purging out bitterness, effacing miseries.

I have what I yearned for—
The chance to live my life out to the end.
And it is a great joy to sit here quietly and think
That soon I shall return to her and say:
'Now it is a free man that kisses you'.
There will be strange meetings in cities for me,
The hush of summer in English gardens,
The glitter of spring in Italy,
The old cafés in Paris.

And I shall have books again,
Long quiet evenings by the tranquil lamp,
Or wild gaiety with 'my own sort'—
And always there will be her love,
Her eyes holding me dumb,
Her mouth drawing the blood to my lips.

And yet and yet
I am still not free from bitterness,
For as I sit here thinking so tenderly of her,
Maybe, over there across the Channel,
Her eyes smile at another man
As they smiled at me,
And her red mouth stabs him to passion
As it stabbed me.
Is any woman both beautiful and loyal?

I think also that I am too restless
For the old life,
Too contemptuous of narrow shoulders
To sit again with the café-chatterers,
Too sick at heart with overmuch slaughter
To dream quietly over books,
Too impatient of lies to cajole
Even my scanty pittance from the money-vultures.

Perhaps, then, this is my happiest moment,
Here in this cold little Belgian house,
Remembering harsh years past,
Plotting gold years to come,
Trusting so blithely in a woman's faith;
In the quiet night,
In the silence.

[*Images of Desire*, 1919]

Two Impressions

I

The colourless morning glides upward
Over the marsh and ragged trees.

Though our mood be sombre
And our bodies angry for more sleep,
This feathered softness of pale light,
Falling negligently upon us,
Delights us.

II

High above the drab barren ground
Three herons beat across the dawn-blue sky.
They drift slowly away
Until they appear
As three horizontal umber brush-strokes
On finely shaded cobalt.
And the mist, driven by the wind
Up and across the distant hill,
Gleams like soft white hair
Brushed amorously backward!

[*Poetry: A Magazine of Verse,* Vol. 14, No. 4,
July 1919. One of the poems belonging to a
group of poems entitled "In France (1916–
1918)". Gates, 1964, 266–67.]

Compensation

As I dozed in a chilly dug-out
I dreamt that Li-Taï-Pé, the sage,
And Sappho, the divine Lesbian,
And Abou-Nawas, the friend of Khalifs,
Came to me saying:
"There can be no death of beauty;
Endure—we also suffered."

And for a token of their love they gave me
A gold chrysanthemum, a fiery rose,
And a cleft-open, dew-sweet nectarine.

[*Poetry: A Magazine of Verse,* Vol. 14, No.
4, July 1919. One of the poems belonging
to a group of poems entitled "In France
(1916–1918)." Gates, 1974, 267.]

Epilogue

Back we go to the shell-tossed land,
To the whine of the shells that tears one's nerves
And the crash that's only not near enough;
Back we go to struggle with mud,
To stumble and slip on the greasy boards,
Back we go to the stink of the dead,
Back we go to the sleepless days
And the unwashed weeks and the mouldy months,
Back we go to the thirst and the dust,
Back we go to the grim despair
That holds a man by the heart in France.

We'll go through it all, the fear and pain,
The breaking up of body and soul,
Take our chance of death after all,
Of face or limb or shoulder smashed,
Go through hell again, face it out,
For her, for her love, for her kiss again.

118

Sneer or snarl, drivel or boast—
What does it matter to us who go
Where they who send us dare not go?
All one to us are the rights and wrongs,
The nations' squabbles, the nations' lies;
Not one land more than another land
Do we love, lovers of love not land—
So it's up the line and hell and pain
For her, for her love, for her kiss again.

[*War and Love (1915–1918),* 1919. Gates, 1974, 288.]

War is an Anachronism

(Sir Toby: Here's an overweening rogue!
Fabian: O, peace. . . .)

The American ladies
Decide war is an anachronism
And that there is no war
The American ladies are amazed
At their own magnanimity
The American financiers
Want to squeeze the last drop of Europe's blood
Before they have another war
So they praise the American ladies
And the ignorant and barbarous Europeans
Wish vaguely that the American ladies
Had made their decision in 1914.

In the next (American) war
What will the American ladies do?
Will they defeat the enemy with resolutions
Will they engulf the rebellious Senate
Will they produce Peace like able conjurers
From short-sleeved shirt waists?
On the contrary
The pacific American ladies

Will intrigue safe jobs in uniform for their lovers
And hand white feathers to other men
(especially if they fought in the German war
And became fed up in the process)
And make wonderful speeches about the cowardice
And cold-blooded neutrality of the British
Who care about nothing but money
And the well-known ferocity of Oriental races
Who are worse than savages and Huns.
And thus shall the wisdom of the New World
Reign supreme and secure o'er Chaos.

[Gates, 1974, 222–23.]

Happiness

It seemed if we might be elsewhere
We might be happy. . . .

A year ago tonight
I lay in a small damp hole
Dug in the brown mud of a sunken road
And shivered (for I had no coat)
Through long cold hours,
And watched the misty stars
And listened for the shells.

What did I feel that night
Beside the cold and a few shells?
Something, something that was good to have,
Something that struggled in my weary mind
Like a child in a tired womb.
Nothing that could be made into philosophy
But just a happy mood.

It was not because the battle was over
Or because I had come through safely,
Or because it was rumoured
That the general said I had done my work well,

Or even because the shells stopped
And the dawn was getting near.
It was none of those things;
And I was too cold and hungry and sleepy
To think clearly.
It came somehow from the stars,
And the slice of moon over the hill,
The black autumn wood in the distance
And from the dark bodies of sleeping men
Who looked, in the thin moonlight,
As if all were dead but the sentries and myself.

I went up the road
(They were still shelling my part)
And looked at the mist in the valley,
Lying flat between the two hills
Like cream in a rough brown bowl.
I went down the road
And talked to the doctor who was awake;
We told each other lies about the battle.

That night I think I was happy
Because I was so aware of beauty,
So sure that what we do matters so little,
So certain I loved and was worth loving,
Certain, for the first time, that I was no exile
But quite friendly with life, especially the stars
And the deep valley and the sleeping men;
Certain I had a right to live.

[Gates, 1974, 184–85.]

Happiness

Not that the battle was over,
Not that we had won and I safe,
Not that the last battery was silent,
Not that I was too tired for misery,
Not from these came happiness—
But from the stars, the dusky moon,

The black distant autumn wood,
The dark bodies of sleeping men in the moonlight
As if all but the sentries were dead.

Happiness struggled in my weary soul
Like a child in the strained womb.

The mist lay in the valley,
Flat between two hills,
Like cream in a rough brown bowl.
We talked in whispers of the battle,
And the frost and the casualties . . .

How can I speak it,
How stab you with my certainties?
That night I was at peace,
Sharply aware of beauty,
Poised, confident, tolerant, at ease,
One that had conquered others and himself,
One that had paid full fee for happiness.

[*The Living Age,* Vol. 312, 21 January 1922. This
poem and the previous longer one with the same
title are clearly related. Gates, 1974, 273.]

Eumenides

It is at night one thinks,
At night, staring with sleepless eyes
At the narrow moonlit room.
Outside the owls hoot briefly,
And there are stars
Whose immortal order makes one shudder.

I do not need the ticking of my watch
To tell me I am mortal;
I have lived with, fed upon death
As happier generations feed on life;
My very mind seems gangrened.

What am I, lying here so still,
Staring till I almost see the silence?
What am I?
What obscure fragment of will?
What paltry life cell?

Have I not striven and striven for health?
Lived calmly (as it seemed) these many months,
Walked daily among neat hedged fields,
Watched the long pageant of the clouds,
Loved, drawn into my being, flowers,
English flowers—the thin anemones,
The honey drops of tufted primroses,
Wild scented hyacinths, white stitchwort,
The spotted orchis, tall scentless violets,
Larch buds, green and scarlet,
Noted the springing green
Of white ash, birch and heavy oak,
Lived with the noblest books, the noblest friends,
Looked gay, laughed free, worked long?

I have done all this,
And yet there are always nights
I lie awake staring with sleepless eyes,
And what is my mind's sickness,
What the agony I struggle with,
I can hardly tell.

Loos, that horrible night in Hart's Crater,
The damp cellars of Maroc,
The frozen ghostly streets of Vermelles,
The first night-long gas bombardment—
O the thousand images I see
And struggle with and cannot kill—
That boot I kicked
(It had a mouldy foot in it)
The night K's head was smashed
Like a rotten pear by a mortar,
The other night I trod on the dead man
And all the officers were hit . . .

These, like Eumenides, glide about me,
Fearful memories of despair and misery,
Tortured flesh, caked blood, endurance,
Men, men and the roar of shells,
The hissing lights, red, green, yellow,
The clammy mud, the tortuous wire,
The slippery boards . . .

It is all so stale,
It has been said a thousand times;
Millions have seen it, been it, as I;
Millions may be haunted by these spirits
As I am haunted;
May feel, as I feel, in the darkness,
Their flesh dripping into corruption,
Their youth and love and gaiety
Dissolved, violently slain, annihilated.

What is it I agonise for?
The dead? They are quiet;
They can have no complaint.
No, it is my own murdered self—
A self which had its passion for beauty,
Some moment's touch with immortality—
Violently slain, which rises up like a ghost
To torment my nights,
To pain me,
It is myself that is the Eumenides,
That will not be appeased, about my bed;
It is the wrong that has been done me
Which none has atoned for, none repented of,
Which rises before me, demanding atonement.

Tell me, what answer shall I give my murdered self?

[*Exile and Other Poems*, 1923]

124

In the Palace Garden

The yews became a part of me,
The long walks edged with sparse flowers,
The fluttering green fringes of elm trees
Blurring the washed blue sky,
The long shivering ripples of the river,
Bird-calls, all we saw and did,
Became me, built me up,
Helped me to love you.
I was happy.
It was enough not to be dead,
Not to be a black spongy mass of decay
Half-buried on the edge of a trench,
More than enough to be young and gay,
To know my lips were such
Yours would be glad to meet them.
I loved you with my old miseries
Which were no longer miseries,
With the scent of lilacs
And the softly sprinkling fountain,
And the kind glances of passers.
How did it happen then?
The sun did not cease shining,
The water rippled just as fleetly,
I loved you just as indiscreetly—
But gradually my golden mood tarnished,
Happiness hissed into nothing—
Metal under a fierce acid—
And I was whispering:
'This happiness is not yours;
It is stolen from other men.
Coward! You have shirked your fate'.

[*Exile and Other Poems*, 1923]

Bones

Now when this coloured curious web
Which hides my awkward bones from sight
Unrolls, and when the thing that's I—
A pinch of lighted dust that flashes—
Has somehow suddenly gone out,
What quaint adventures may there be
For my unneeded skeleton?

Some men's bones are left (like trees
Which cannot move from where they root)
On open hills or low damp hollows,
Wherever war has struck them down;
And some bones after many years
A waggish bomb digs up, and strews—
Thigh bones and ribs mixed up with coffins—
About a well-bombarded town;
And some are plunged with ancient wreckage
Where fishes with blue bulging eyes

Slide past, and clouds of tiniest shells
In ages make a rocky cover;
And some lie here and some lie there
Until they moulder quite away;
Some in the village garth and some
In quiet suburban labelled rows;
And some are powdered up in fire
And some are shown in dull museums. . . .

Now, while his flesh remains, a man
Is something; but who feels akin
To any nameless poor old bones?
Even she, who with miraculous lips
Set little flowering plots of kisses
Over our body, will not care
To hug us when our bones are dry;
And she who carried us nine months
And built them with her vital blood
Might pass them by and never know
These were the bones so hard to bear;

And likelier still, our dearest child
Would scorn to know us so unveiled,
Unwilling to believe his flesh,
Still firm and petal-sweet, was bred
By such a pitiful old wreck.

But, in the end, the bones go too,
And drift about as dust which hangs
In a long sun-shaft, or dissolve
Into the air to help build up
The pulpy tissues of fine leaves
Or heavier flakes of ruddy flesh,
Or even someone else's bones.

I leave to those superior minds
Who make theology their care
The task of settling whose shall be
These much-used frameworks at the last;
I rather see a wearier world
Shed, aeons hence, its comely flesh
To dance, a mournful skeleton,
Sedately round a dingier sun.

[*Exile and Other Poems*, 1923]

The Faun Complains[95]

They give me aeroplanes
Instead of birds and moths;
Instead of sunny fields
They give me mud-holes;
And for my day-long, night-long sacred hush,
(Flutter of leaves, bee-murmurs in the flowers,
Ripe seeded grass just stirring into music)
A hush wherein one seemed to hear
The invisible wheels of burning stars
Echoing upon the tiled paths of heaven—
For this they give me noise,
Harsh clangours of breaking metal,
Abrupt huge bursts of flame.

And for my woodland playmates,
Dryads,[96] yellow subtle fauns,
Naked wanton hamadryads,
And stealthy water-girls
Who stole my honey and fruits
When I lay sleeping by their pools—
For these they give me men,
Odd, loud-voiced, fearsome men,
Who mock my little horns and pointed ears!

[*Collected Poems*. New York: Covici, Friede,
1928. Gates, 1974, 323.]

Epilogue to *Death of a Hero*

Eleven years after the fall of Troy,
We, the old men—some forty of us nearly forty—
Met and talked on the sunny rampart
Over our wine, while the lizards scuttled
In dusty grass, and the crickets chirred.

Some bared their wounds;
Some spoke of the thirst, dry in the throat,
And the heart-beat, in the din of battle;
Some spoke of intolerable sufferings,
The brightness gone from their eyes
And the grey already thick in their hair.

And I sat a little apart
From the garrulous talk and old memories,
And I heard a boy of twenty
Say petulantly to a girl, seizing her arm:
"Oh, come away; why do you stand there
Listening open-mouthed to the talk of old men?
Haven't you heard enough of Troy and Achilles?
Why should they bore us for ever
With an old quarrel and the names of dead men
We never knew, and dull forgotten battles?"

And he drew her away,
And she looked back and laughed
As he spoke more contempt of us,
Being now out of hearing.

And I thought of the graves by desolate Troy
And the beauty of many young men now dust,
And the long agony, and how useless it all was.
And the talk still clashed about me
Like the meeting of blade and blade.

And as they two moved further away
He put an arm about her, and kissed her;
And afterwards I heard their gay distant laughter.

And I looked at the hollow cheeks
And the weary eyes and the grey-streaked heads
Of the old men—nearly forty—about me;
And I too walked away
In an agony of helpless grief and pity.

[This poem comes at the end of *Death of a Hero*, 1929, 439–40.]

In Memory of Wilfred Owen

I had half-forgotten among the soft blue waters
And the gay-fruited arbutus of the hill
Where never the nightingales are silent,
And the sunny hours are warm with honey and dew;

I had half-forgotten as the stars slid westward
Year after year in grave majestic order,
In the strivings and in the triumphs of manhood,
The world's voice, and the touch of beloved hands.

But I have never quite forgotten, never forgotten
All you who lie there so lonely, and never stir
When the hired buglers call unheeded to you,
Whom the sun shall never warm nor the frost chill.

Do you remember . . . but why should you remember?
Have you not given all you had, to forget?
Oh, blessed, blessed be Death! They can no more vex you,
You for whom memory and forgetfulness are one.

1931

[*The Eaten Heart*, 1933]

By the King's Most Excellent Majesty

A Proclamation

1914

don't want to lose you
    you ought to go
your King and your Country
      kiss you
when you come back

1915

    a long way
it's a long way to go
    a long way
goodbye   farewell
it's a long long way

1916

I want to go home
    home
take me over the sea
don't want to die
    home

1917

take the cylinders out of my kidneys
the connecting rod out of my brain
    from under my backbone
assemble   again

1918

I know where they are,
    where they are
    on the old barbed wire
I've seen them I've seen them
hanging on the old barbed wire
I've seen

1919

and when I die
don't bury me at all
just pickle my bones
in alcohol
    in al-co-hol

GOD SAVE THE KING

[This poem appears at the beginning of
Part II of Aldington's 1933 novel, *All Men
are Enemies*, 124–25]

Death of Another Hero

Who is this that is borne with lamentation,
Who is this that is honoured by a proud people?
Is it one who gave life and hope?
Is it one who gave knowledge, wisdom or beauty?
Is it one who died that others might live?
Who is this hero? Let me know,
Let me share in the sorrow of my nation
And lay my wreath of praise on a worthy tomb.

It is the rich man who is dead at last,
Struck—Nemesis!—in the very brain
Which plotted all that senseless gathering.

Gone! Like a beggar, like a frowsty worm
Trodden beneath the contemptuous foot of Death.

It is the rich man, he who spent the years,
All lovely hours or dark, to gather more,
And yet more, and yet more, and more and more,
He who possessed, who was feared, who was hated,
Crucified himself between conceit and fear,
Now boasting of his power like a loud pimp
Bullying a frightened woman, and anon,
His eyes darkened and narrowed with fear,
Dreading in abject bowel-shaken terror
The speechless vengeance of the wronged.

It is the rich man, peak-quotation Judas,
Who for five hundred-million silver pieces
Sold life and his fellow men,
But first and last and every day himself,
And with each shilling bought a sullen fear,
The fear of losing it.

Now all are lost.

Ring out, base bugles! Sound, ye empty drums!
Stand to attention, low Servility,
Lick-spittle Flattery, whining Parasites!
Your hero passes. Stand with palms reversed
And pockets inside out.
And you, gaunt legions of the too-honoured slain,
Rise from your geometric lines of graves,
Kindle in empty sockets the fierce fires
Of your avenging eyes, stare from your shrouds,
There goes your general to his last unrest,
There trails one corpse which made you corpses too.

[*The Poems of Richard Aldington*, 1934]

NOTES

94. Barlow, 1987, 8.
95. Both H. D. and Ezra Pound referred to Aldington as a "faun."
96. "Dryad" was Pound's nickname for H.D.

132

Part III
Prose Poems

Most of the prose poems that comprise this section are taken from *The Love of Myrrhine and Konallis, and Other Prose Poems*, 1926. In turn, many of these are reused in the short story "Farewell to Memories" in *Roads to Glory*, 1930. Only the second version of "Escape" appears here in prose lineation. All the others are in the form of free verse.

Aldington's four major themes are present once more: the harsh reality of war, an idealized classical past, love of nature, and love of woman. And, as before, it is the last three that offer the opportunity to escape in memory, imagination and wish-fulfillment from the first.

In "Discouragement" Aldington deprecatingly explains his choice of the prose poem as a means of expression. Because his individual voice and personality have been submerged and stifled by the pressure to behave as part of a single-minded mass, he feels unable to attempt disciplined originality, and too feeble to "dare the cool / rhythm of prose, the sharp / edges of poetry." All he can manage is "some humble poem in prose."

In "Fatigues" the poet is one of a gang of men employed in unloading bales of hay for the horses. The work is hot, dirty, and exhausting. Escape into a remembered English pastoral is occasioned by the scents that come from the bundles they heave around. A litany of wild flowers from the hedgerows and meadows of English and Welsh counties lifts his spirit above the aching tiredness that invades his limbs. These cherished bales must be treated with great love and tenderness because they recall not only the scents and sights of an English summer, but also, by extension, the fragility of feminine beauty: "I stoop and kiss you / furtively. No one sees. / Dear gentle perished sisters, speak, / whisper and move, tell me you will / dance and whisper for me in the / wind next June."

In "Sorcery of Words" Aldington manipulates the cliché "the poetry of winter" backwards and forwards in time and space. The poet recalls having first read the words as an abstract generalization in some academic essay. He then applies the phrase to a recent concrete occurrence, namely, the wintry landscape he woke up to at dawn yesterday. He ponders the fact that it is indeed possible to appreciate "the poetry of winter" even when one's physical circumstances mitigate against such a response, in this instance when he was "hungry, sore, unshaven, dirty," "aching," and "shivering." In the final six lines he transfers his thoughts back to a comfortable peacetime library in England where he urges a putative reader to attempt to catch and comprehend the true meaning of the phrase, "The poetry of winter."

The state of the poet's hands in "Our Hands" could well be the result of the kind of manual labor outlined in "Fatigues." Hands, which are normally one of the means through which human beings make contact with various manifestations of beauty, have been harshened by the degrading routine of army life. Hands, which were "reverent" when they came into contact with "roses and / women's flesh, old lovely books and / marbles of Carrara," "tressed hair and silken robe and / gentle fingers," and "bronze and wood and stone and / rustling parchment," are now observed by the poet with sadness and pity.

"The Road" has a tripartite structure. In the opening section the poet transports us back to ancient Greece. He would gladly have been kept awake all night by the chance to hear Socrates speak. The exhilaration of such a transcendental experience would have banished tiredness. The long central section abandons this exalted mood and replaces it with a low-keyed monotony, the repetitious automaton-like quality of movement of men and the machinery of war up and down the "Road" (perhaps Aldington has in mind the notorious Menin Road). The darkness of night offers some protection to the constant traffic, this "harsh monotonous epic." The one moment of colour in this bleak monochrome landscape comes when "sharp bullets strike gold sparks" from the cobbles on the Road. This image also occurs in "Machine Guns": "Gold sparks / where the fierce bullets strike the stones." In the final section, just as dawn breaks, this nocturnal military traffic is replaced in the poet's imagination by a never-ending march past of the ghosts of the dead of all the warring nations. They "march down," "march back, / march home."

"Stand-To" is predicated on a series of contrasts: night and dawn, light and dark, a rat and a lark, dirt and cleanliness, guilt and innocence. At the end the poet has a fantastic vision: "Out of the east as from a temple / comes a procession of girls and young / men, smiling brave, candid, / ignorant of grief." Only

136

those with firsthand experience of the anguish of darkness and night (i.e. war) will be able to appreciate fully the light and beauty of dawn (i.e. peace).

In "In an Old Battlefield" Aldington seamlessly integrates a number of his themes. It is also one of his bleakest and most pessimistic poems. The opening assertion, "Life has deceived us," is followed by no redemptive aspects of life. Everything is marked by staleness and oblivion: thoughts, beautiful objects, even the war's horrors: "all this was old,—/ a thousand times felt and forgotten." At the end of the poem the poet is skeptical even about the love of a woman. He wonders in fact whether her kiss, breast, and hands were, in turn: "the reflection of dead kisses," "a common thing," "a worn memory of hands crumbled into cool dust." This chilly poem provides us perhaps with some glimpses of Aldington's state of mind and nerves at the end of the war.

In "Escape" the poet fantasizes about one of his favorite means of evading the grim reality of war, by entering the imagined and idealized tranquillity of the classical world. The angry rhetoric is equally strong in both versions. Aldington has chosen to omit some material present in the letter version, perhaps feeling it was redundant, verged on cliché, or was too abstract, e.g. "monstrous sin," "the chains of restraint," "fetid striations," "resentment and trickery and slavishness." He also cut the final three lines, presumably for being unnecessarily explanatory.

"Landscape" is a deceptive poem. For much of it we are lulled into a false sense of peace, beauty, and optimism. The cleansing action of moonlight and a fresh breeze are apparently beginning to modify, beautify, and even remove the evidence of death and destruction. The effect being produced is likened to the purity of an idealized Greek location: "the marble / rock of some Greek island, piercing / its sparse garment of lavenders and / mints like a naked nymph among / rustling leaves." Just as we are about to protest at this incongruous and absurdly escapist fantasy, Aldington cuts the ground from under our feet with a piece of brutal, down-to-earth realism. In the final six lines the sweet smell in the air is not in fact newly mown hay, but "phosgene. . . . / And tomorrow there will be huddled / corpses with blue horrible faces / and foam on their writhed mouths."

In "Dawns" Aldington begins by stating that although he can remember some peacetime dawns in the Italian towns of Florence and Ravello, and in London after a night of lovemaking, he is haunted by other dawns, "tragic and pitiful." These are wartime dawns that he experienced in shattered barns or in the trenches. Both categories of dawns are recalled with pin-sharp visual, auditory and tactile details: "lips and eyes heavy with many kisses," "cool waves / of light gliding over the silvery roofs / of London," "the first sparrows twittered in the heavy plane trees," "the sterile glitter of snow," and "one's breath was frozen to the blanket." The final wartime dawn is the most clearly etched in his mind's eye. As night gradually gives way to wan daylight he sees a stretcher party "silhouetted / against the whitening east," "sharply edged / in black on that smooth sky." The burdens they carry are dead soldiers: "And as / the groups passed they shouted the / names of the things they carried—/ things which yesterday were / living men." In the final lines Aldington's duty as an officer in these circumstances is expressed in a laconic throwaway manner, similar in effect to the ending of 'Soliloquy–2": "And I forwarded my report through / the usual channels."

Both "The Return" and "In the Library" convey some sense of the alienation Aldington felt on his return to England and of the difficulty of adjusting to life after the war. The words that give us the key to Aldington's feeling of being a superfluous man, of his existential angst, are: "alien," "repulsion," "exasperates," "shrinks away," and "purposeless triviality." In "In the Library" his efforts to turn once more to his beloved Greek are frustrated. He cannot immerse himself in study of and delight in the classics. Trench memories keep surfacing to obliterate the pleasure of Greek verse. In each of these prose poems Aldington's knowledge of the classics supplies him with a helpful simile as he seeks to explain his torment: "Like Odysseus, fresh from the bloody / sacrifice to the cold ghosts, I bear / with me a flavour of the grave, a / rebuke from the unremembered dead," and "I am . . . / weary as the lost Argonauts beating / hopelessly for home against the / implacable storm."

In "Bodies" war flashbacks interrupt his lovemaking. Even the close physical presence of his beloved's naked body cannot stave off the "ghastly memories." This particular memory concerns the discovery and removal for burial of two rotting, stinking corpses in a house in a French village. The poem ends with the poet's unspoken plea: "Let me not shriek out—let me hide my / face in your breasts and shudder a / little and try to forget."

Fatigues

The weariness of this dirt and labour,
　　of this dirty melting sky!
For hours we have carried great bundles
　　of hay from barge to truck and
　　from truck to train. . . .
The weariness of this dirt and labour!
But look! Last June those heavy dried
　　bales waved and glittered in the
　　fields of England.
Cinque-foil and clover, buttercups,
　　fennel, thistle and rue, daisy and
　　ragged robin, wild rose from the
　　hedge, shepherd's purse, and long
　　sweet nodding stalks of grass.
Heart of me, heart of me, be not sick
　　and faint, though fingers and arms
　　and head ache; you bear the gift
　　of the glittering meadows of
　　England. Here are bundles from
　　Somerset, from Wales, from
　　Hereford, Worcester, Gloucester—
　　names we must love, scented with
　　summer peace.
Handle them bravely, meadow-sweet,
　　sorrel, lush flag and arid knap-weed,
　　flowers of marsh and cliff,
　　handle them bravely.
Dear crushed flowers, and you, yet
　　fragrant grasses, I stoop and kiss you
　　furtively. No one sees.
Dear gentle perished sisters, speak,
　　whisper and move, tell me you will
　　dance and whisper for me in the
　　wind next June.

Base Camp, Calais, 1916

[*Images of War: A Book of Poems*. London: C.W. Beaumont, 1919.
The Love of Myrrhine and Konallis, and Other Prose Poems,
1926. With slight alterations, in the short story "Farewell to
Memories" in *Roads to Glory*, 1930. Gates 1974, 307–8.]

Sorcery of Words

"The poetry of winter"—these words,
 remembered from some aesthetic
 essay, return and return to my
 memory, with an ironic persistence.
 It happened yesterday when the
 ground was sheeted in frost, the sky
 rose upon the pale green coverlet of
 dawn, bare trees silhouetted, frozen
 pools of water.
"The poetry of winter"—yes, that was
 indeed poetry, the breath of the
 gods, light glowing and changing,
 motionless trees, clear air.
Yes, one can be hungry, sore, unshaven,
 dirty, eyes and head aching, limbs
 shivering, and yet love beauty.
From the depths I cry it, from the
 depths which echo with the ironic
 phrase "the poetry of winter",
 from the depths I cry it!
You, who are clean and warm with the
 delicate leisure of a flower-scented
 library, strain your hearing, listen
 across the clamour of the age, for a
 whisper that comes to you so faintly,
 so ironically—"The poetry of winter."

Base Camp, Calais, 1917

[*Reverie: A Little Book of Poems for H.D.,* 1917. *Images of War: A Book of Poems.* London: C.W. Beaumont, 1919. *The Love of Myrrhine and Konallis, and Other Prose Poems,* 1926. Also in the short story, "Farewell to Memories" in *Roads to Glory,* 1930. Gates, 1974, 308–9.]

Our Hands

I am grieved for our hands
    that have caressed roses and
    women's flesh, old lovely books and
    marbles of Carrara. I am grieved for
    our hands that were so reverent in
    beauty's service, so glad of beauty of
    tressed hair and silken robe and
    gentle fingers, so glad of beauty of
    bronze and wood and stone and
    rustling parchment. So glad,
    so reverent, so white.
I am grieved for our hands.

1917

[*The Egoist*, Vol. 4, No. 8, (September 1917). *Reverie: A Little Book of Poems for H.D.*, 1917. *Images of War: A Book of Poems*. London: C.W. Beaumont, 1919. *The Love of Myrrhine and Konallis, and Other Prose Poems*, 1926. Gates, 1974, 309.]

The Road

To have watched all night at the feast
    where Socrates spoke of love,
    letting fall from tranquil fingers
    white violets in the cool black wine;
    or to have listened while some
    friend of Bembo talked of the graves
    of Academe and made golden flesh
    for us the ghosts of dead Greece—
    who would shrink from so exquisite
    a vigil? Then indeed not to sleep
    would be divine, the dawn—the first
    birds among the trees in the misty
    park, the first gold flush—would fill
    us perhaps with regret, certainly
    with exaltation.
But there is no exaltation for those who
    watch beside the Road, the Road

some know too bitterly and some
will never know, the Road which is
the Place of Skulls—for it starts
from a graveyard and passes through
graveyards and ends in a graveyard.
By day the Road is empty and desolate;
no boot or wheel marks its mud,
no human figure is reflected in its
deep shell-pools. By day the Road is
silent. But by night it is alive with a
harsh monotonous epic. Along that
muddy trail move the rattling
transport limbers, the field-guns, the
ammunition wagons, the Red-Cross
cars lurch and sway on their springs
over its deep ruts. Down the Road
come the weary battalions, platoon
after platoon, heroic in their
mud and silence. Down that Road
come the dead men on their silent
wheeled stretchers. All that goes up
that Road is strong and young and
alive; all that comes down is weary
and old or dead. Over that Road
shriek and crash the shells; the
sharp bullets strike gold sparks from
its stones; the mortars tear craters
in it. And just before dawn when
the last limber rattles away and the
last stretcher has gone back to the
line, then the ghosts of the dead
armies march down, heroic in their
silence, battalion after battalion,
brigade after brigade, division after
division; the immeasurable forces of
the dead youth of Europe march
down the Road past the silent sentry,
past the ruined house, march back,
march home.

Maroc, 1917

[*The Egoist*, Vol. 5, No. 7 (August 1918). *The Love of Myrrhine and Konallis, and Other Prose Poems,* 1926. Also, minus a few lines, in the short story "Farewell to Memories" in *Roads to Glory*, 1930. Gates, 1974, 314–16.]

Discouragement

To have passed so close to annihilation
    and (which is worse) to have become
    stained so inalterably with the ideas
    and habits of masses—this leaves me
    immeasurably discouraged, out of
    love with myself.
Now I am good only to mimic inferior
    masters. My thoughts are stifling—
    heavy grey dust from a scorched road.
For me silence; or if speech, then some
    humble poem in prose. Indeed I am
    too conscientious—or shall we say
    too impotent?—to dare the cool
    rhythm of prose, the sharp
    edges of poetry.
    Nymphes de Parnasse!
    Encore un Pégase raté!

Officers' Camp, Fressin, 1918

[*Poetry: A Magazine of Verse*, Vol. 13, No. 11 (November 1918). *The Love of Myrrhine and Konallis, and Other Prose Poems,* 1926. Parts of it also appear in the short story "Farewell to Memories" in *Roads to Glory*, 1930. Gates, 1974, 306–7.]

Stand-To

Slowly, too slowly, the night, with its
    noise and its fear and its murder,
    yields to the dawn. One by one the
    guns cease. Quicker, O dawn,
    quicker—dazzle the hateful stars,
    lighten for us the weight of
    the shadows.
The last rat scuttles away; the first
    lark thrills with a beating of wings
    and song. The light is soft;
    deliberately, consciously, the young
    dawn moves. My unclean flesh is
    penetrated with her sweetness and
    she does not disdain even me.
Out of the east as from a temple
    comes a procession of girls and young
    men, smiling, brave, candid,
    ignorant of grief.
Few men know the full bitterness of
    night, but they alone will know the
    full beauty of dawn—if
    dawn ever comes.

Loos, 1918

[*Poetry: A Magazine of Verse*, Vol. 13, No. 11 (November 1918).
The Love of Myrrhine and Konallis, and Other Prose Poems,
1926. Also in the short story "Farewell to Memories" in *Roads to
Glory*, 1930. Gates, 1974, 310.]

In an Old Battlefield

Life has deceived us. The thoughts we
    found so vivid and fresh were dull
    and crass as the prayers muttered to
    a worn rosary by an infidel priest.
The joy we felt in beauty, our sense

144

of discovery at the touch of some
age-green bronze; even the sick
horror of some battlefield where the
flesh had not quite fallen from the
shattered bones—all this was old,—
a thousand times felt and forgotten.
And is the kiss of your mouth then
but the reflection of dead kisses,
the gleam of your breast a common
thing? Was the touch of your hand
but a worn memory of hands
crumbled into cool dust?

Loos, 1918.

[*Poetry: A Magazine of Verse*, Vol. 13, No. 11 (November 1918).
The Love of Myrrhine and Konallis, and Other Prose Poems,
1926. Also, minus the last six lines, in the short story "Farewell
to Memories" in *Roads to Glory*, 1930. Gates, 1974, 311.]

Escape

Escape, let the soul escape from this
insanity, this insult to God, from this
ruined landscape, these murdered
fields, this bitterness, this agony,
from this harsh death and disastrous
mutilation, from this filth and labour,
this stench of bodies and
unwashed living bodies—escape,
let the soul escape!
Let the soul escape and move with
emotion along ilex walks under a
quiet sky. There, lingering for a while
beside the marble head of some
shattered Hermes, it strews the
violets of regret for a lost loveliness
as transient as itself. Or perhaps by
some Homeric sea, watching the

145

crisp foam blown by a straight wind,
it gathers sea-flowers, exquisite in
their restraint of colour and
austere sparseness of petal.
There, perhaps, among flowers,
at twilight, under the glimmer of
the first stars, it will find a
sensation of a quiet almost kindly
universe, indifferent to this
festering activity.

Loos, 1918

[*Poetry: A Magazine of Verse*, Vol. 13, No. 11 (November 1918).
The Love of Myrrhine and Konallis, and Other Prose Poems,
1926. The first nine lines also appear in the short story "Farewell
to Memories" in *Roads to Glory*, 1930. Gates, 1974, 312–13.]

Escape

Escape, escape! From the monstrous sin of this insanity, from
the chains of restraint, from this ruined landscape, these mur-
dered fields, these fetid striations across the body of earth, from
this insult to God, this murder & bitterness & agony, from this
harsh metallic death & more disastrous mutilation, from this
filth and this labour, this stench of unwashed bodies, this resent-
ment & trickery & slavishness—escape, escape!

Let the soul escape & move with emotion along ilex walls in
the company of lyric women, with tenderness, with delicacy.
There, lingering for a while beside the marble head of some shat-
tered Hermes it strews the violets of regret for a lost loveliness
as transient as itself. There, perhaps, by some Homeric sea it
watches the crisp foam of a straight wind & gathers sea flowers
exquisite in their acrid restraint of colour & austere sparseness
of petal.

There, remote from turbulence, it lies at twilight among flow-
ers that simulate the drooping asphodel and at the first glimmer
of frail stars it catches for a moment some [inkling] of harmony,
a sensation of a quiet, almost kindly universe, indifferent to [the
festering] activity [of perverted intelligence.]

146

Yes, the escape is perfect & complete; the spirit moves more easily from the flesh, hoping eagerly for some complete separation which will render it all liberty & return to it that tranquillity which formerly it enjoyed as a right.[97]

Landscape

The moon, high-seated above the
    ridge, fills the ruined village with
    tranquil light and black broken
    shadows—ruined walls, shattered
    timbers, piles of rubbish, torn-up
    ground, almost beautiful in this
    radiance, in this quiet June air.
Somehow to-night the air blows
    cleaner and sweeter—the chemistry
    of earth is slowly putrefying the
    corrupting bodies, the waste and
    garbage of armies. Sweetness,
    darkness, clean space—the marble
    rock of some Greek island, piercing
    its sparse garment of lavenders and
    mints like a naked nymph among
    rustling leaves.
Heavy scented the air tonight—
    new-mown hay—a pungent exotic
    odour—phosgene. . . .
And to-morrow there will be huddled
    corpses with blue horrible faces
    and foam on their writhed mouths.

                Loos, May, 1918

[*Poetry: A Magazine of Verse*, Vol. 13, No. 11 (November 1918). *The Love of Myrrhine and Konallis, and Other Prose Poems*, 1926. Also in the short story "Farewell to Memories" in *Roads to Glory*, 1930. Gates, 1974, 314.]

Dawns

I am haunted by the memory of my dawns.
  Not those earlier dawns when I saw
  for the first time the bell-towers of
  Florence in the lucid air, of the hills
  of Ravello violet and mist-wreathed
  against the gold sky; not those dawns
  when I rose from some exquisite and
  beloved body, the brain still feverish
  with desire, lips and eyes heavy with
  many kisses, to watch the cool waves
  of light gliding over the silvery roofs
  of London whilst the first sparrows
  twittered in the heavy plane-trees.
  Not those dawns, but others,
  tragic and pitiful.
I remember those harsh wakenings
  of winter-time in old French barns
  through whose broken tiles at night
  one saw the morose glitter of the
  stars and at dawn the sterile glitter
  of snow, dawn when one's breath
  was frozen to the blanket, and the
  contact of the air was anguish.
I am haunted by sombre or ironically
  lovely dawns seen from some bleak
  parade-ground, by misty spring dawns
  in the trenches, when the vague
  shapes of the wire seemed to be the
  forms of crouching enemies, by
  summer dawns when the fresh
  immeasurably deep blue was a
  blasphemy, an insult to
  human misery.
Yet one among them all is poignant,
  unforgettable. As the shapes of
  things grew out slowly from the
  darkness, and the gentle grey
  suffusion of light made outlines
  visible, little groups of men carrying

stretchers on their shoulders came
slowly, stumbling and hesitating,
along the ruined street. For a
moment each group was silhouetted
against the whitening east: the steel
helmets (like those of mediaeval
men-at-arms), the slung rifles, the
strained postures of carrying, the
useless vacillating corpse under its
sepulchral blanket—all sharply edged
in black on that smooth sky. And as
the groups passed they shouted the
names of the things they carried—
things which yesterday were
living men.
And I forwarded my report through
the usual channels.

Loos, 1918

[*The Egoist*, Vol. 5, No. 9 (October 1918). *The Love of Myrrhine and Konallis, and Other Prose Poems,* 1926. Also, with the omission of a few lines, in the short story "Farewell to Memories" in *Roads to Glory*, 1930. Gates, 1974, 316–17.]

Song

Song—once that meant song indeed:
    the voices of Sappho's nightingales,
    the exultation of beauty
    over-whelming the modesty of silence.
    Once it seemed that all life was song:
    even trivial or base things becoming
    lovely with that passion; even
    death becoming less terrible when
    hidden by sombre and luxuriously
    sad words. For when life was an
    ecstasy of discovery—each day with
    some new gift of beauty—homely

daily speech became song. To have
loved the world for years, with the
immense vividness of new loves—
that was a gift worthy the
imperishable Olympians.

But now that youth has gone, and the
soul stifles in monotonous captivity,
song has come to have a new
meaning—more common but more
pathetic. It has come to mean now
the expression of the grief and
courage and acceptation of fate of
common, poor men. Song—any cheap
ordinary song—becomes strange and
pathetic, when sung by weary
dispirited men.

I remember song which might have
moved even rich women to
understanding and compassion:
twenty men huddled in a leaky tent
singing wistfully of the Devon hills;
a weary platoon marching back
through the ruins of Vermelles,
pitiless in frost and sharp moonlight,
singing as they stumbled along; little
parties of men coming down the line
for leave, singing in almost
hysterical gladness.

Only last night, in the midst of a
raid—searchlights, menacing hum of
planes, soft thuds of anti-aircraft
guns, deep rapidly-nearing crashes
of bombs, no cover—I found three
boys sitting in darkness, softly
singing old tunes.

No longer the sharp edge of Attic
song, but the immeasurable pathos
of the song of common men,
patient under disaster.

Divisional Camp, 1918.

[*The Love of Myrrhine and Konallis, and Other Prose Poems,*
1926. Gates, 1974, 317–19.]

Lethe

Those who have passed through hell
    need only to pass through Lethe to
    become sane once more. When I
    remember those horrible brooding
    years my body shudders; an immense
    discouragement, a brooding weariness
    envelopes me.
Old pain, old terror, old exasperations
    crowd upon me—nights spent in
    shivering anguish shovelling cold
    mud under shell fire; interminable
    marches over pavé roads through
    incredibly insipid country, marches
    when the over-weight of a soldier's
    burden became an exasperation, a
    mad obsession; wet night watches
    in splashy trenches, mud soaking legs
    and feet to a kind of numb pain—
    and always the fierce whine of
    bullets, the nerve-racking detonation
    of shells; exhausting unrefreshing
    sleep in frowsy dug-outs on
    verminous sacks; food muddy and
    impure. And always the menace—
    annihilation. Every second it was
    possible—how did we not go mad?
    We were mad, utterly insane.
Proserpina, Lady of Hell, in whose
    keeping are the great sombre rivers,
    grant me I beseech one draught of
    Lethe to purge my spirit of horror,
    to make me worthy to mingle with
    sane men once more.

London, 1919

[*The Anglo-French Review*, Vol. 1, No. 6 (July 1919). *The Love of Myrrhine and Konallis, and Other Prose Poems,* 1926. Also in the short story "Farewell to Memories" in *Roads to Glory*, 1930. Gates, 1974, 319.]

The Return

How I am alien here! How my
    presence troubles the pleasures of
    those who have not lived in hell!
    Like Odysseus, fresh from the bloody
    sacrifice to the cold ghosts, I bear
    with me a flavour of the grave, a
    rebuke from the unremembered dead.
Even in the crowded streets I carry
    repulsion. Even the pale glitter of
    light upon the wet stones exasperates
    me with its tranquillity; even the
    sallow prostitute, trying to speak to
    me, shrinks away. Like foolish
    mannikins the men I knew hunt in
    a ring some purposeless triviality.
    Only from one hand can I gain life—
    and that hand is denied me.

London, 1919

[*The Love of Myrrhine and Konallis, and Other Prose Poems,* 1926. Gates, 1974, 320.]

In the Library

There is a strange void in my brain.
    I bend over the black-speckled page
    and try to seize its life. What is it
    I am reading? Greek? What does
    Greek matter?

152

The rose-crowns of Anacreon, the
    dances of women eager to be taken,
    the sound of the fluid syllables,
    escape me.
I am out again on the muddy
    trench-boards, wearily trudging along
    those chalky ditches, under the rain,
    under the shells. . . .
I am utterly weary now that it is over,
    weary as the lost Argonauts beating
    hopelessly for home against the
    implacable storm.

London, 1919

[*The Love of Myrrhine and Konallis, and Other Prose Poems,*
1926. Gates, 1974, 320–21.]

Bodies

Your slight body lies on the coloured
    cushions before the fire; red light
    blooms in its shadows and the higher
    curved flesh glows white and gold.
    Your eyes are half shut, your clear
    red lips just parted; under the small
    left breast I see the beating of your
    heart. I sit and watch you as you
    drowse. You are life.
But the horror will not leave me yet;
    for suddenly my senses are filled by
    ghastly memories. I struggle against
    them. Useless. The beauty of your
    body goes, the room, the silence,
    the perfume.
I stand with an old Frenchman by a
    ruined outhouse in a by-street of
    the village.
"Behind that door, Monsieur," he says,

153

"you will find another of them."
The filthy stench of rotten flesh
    assaults my throat and nostrils,
    terrifies the animal in me. I bend—
    as I now bend above you—and note
    the shattered bloody skull, the
    grinning fixed face desecrated with
    dust, blue-grey like the uniform.
    It is a young German officer.
    Someone has taken his boots and his
    stockinged feet stick out ridiculously.
    He was handsome once; how would
    his mistresses like him now?
    Poof! What a stink!
The old man is not moved.
"There is another down the
    street, Monsieur."
"Show me; I will have them buried."
Let me not shriek out—let me hide my
    face in your breasts and shudder a
    little and try to forget.

London, 1919

[*The Anglo-French Review*, Vol. 3, No. 2 (March 1920). *The Love of Myrrhine and Konallis, and Other Prose Poems,* 1926. Gates, 1974, 321–22.]

The Last Salute

We pass and leave you lying. No need
    for rhetoric, for funeral music, for
    melancholy bugle-calls. No need for
    tears now, no need for regret.
We took our risk with you; you died
    and we live. We take your noble
    gifts, salute for the last time those
    lines of pitiable crosses, those solitary
    mounds, those unknown graves and

turn to live our lives out as we may.
Which of us were the fortunate who
   can tell? For you there is silence
   and the cold twilight drooping in
   awful desolation over those
   motionless lands. For us sunlight and
   the sound of women's voices, song
   and hope and laughter; despair,
   gaiety, love—life.
Lost terrible silent comrades, we, who
   might have died, salute you.

London, 1919

[*The Anglo-French Review*, Vol. 1, No. 4 (May 1919). *The Love of Myrrhine and Konallis, and Other Prose Poems,* 1926. Also in the short story "Farewell to Memories" in *Roads to Glory*, 1930. Gates, 1974, 322.]

NOTES

97. Enclosed in a letter to Bryher (Winifred Ellerman) on 1 January 1919. The brackets are Aldington's. Quoted in Zilboorg, 1992, 87–88. In l. 5 Zilboorg has "unmasked" instead of "unwashed." Both *The Love of Myrrhine and Konallis, and Other Prose Poems* and "Farewell to Memories" in *Roads to Glory* give "unwashed."
   98. Hughes, 1931, 99.
   99. *The Complete Poems of Richard Aldington*, 1948, 190.
   100. Barlow, 1987, 14
   101. Zilboorg, 1992, 221.
   102. Gates, 1974, 155.

Part IV
Fragments of Longer Poems

In 1923, Aldington was living in a quiet rural backwater in Berkshire. In his autobiography he describes the cottage in which he lived as a ramshackle structure set against the end wall of an old malthouse. He informs us that during the years 1920–28 he worked almost continuously, read voraciously and, taking his own writing and translation work together, produced about two hundred thousand words a year. He reckons his daily work schedule matched that of any office worker, and that in fact his working day was longer. (243–44) It seems that the distinctly unremarkable quality of his simple surroundings induced him to respond in appropriately old-fashioned verse. He confessed that the valley of the Kennet was low-keyed and homely, but claimed that its charms equalled those of pastoral poetry. (246) In 108 lines "The Berkshire Kennet" celebrates the joys and rewards of this gentle country life, and is written in octosyllabic rhyming couplets, reminiscent, appropriately enough, of eighteenth-century verse.[98] The lulling rhythm and the patiently recorded details of this bucolic idyll (at times very close in form and spirit to parts of Rupert Brooke's "The Old Vicarage, Grantchester") are sufficient to mitigate any memories of war.

Before eventually abandoning poetry to concentrate on prose, Aldington was to develop a tendency, beginning with "The Berkshire Kennet," to write longer, more discursive poems of a philosophical nature. *A Fool i' the Forest* is forty-seven pages long, and is one of Aldington's most ambitious poems. In his introductory note Aldington explains that the three characters, the narrator ("I"), Mezzetin, and the Conjuror, are meant to be read as

one person split into three. "I" is intended to be typical of a man of our own time, one who is by temperament more fitted for an art than a scientific civilisation. He is shown at a moment of crisis, and the phantasmagoria is the mirror of his mind's turmoil as he struggles to attain a harmony between himself and the exterior world.

Mezzetin comes from the *Commedia dell' Arte*. He symbolises here the imaginative faculties—art, youth satire, irresponsible gaiety, liberty. He is one or several of these by turns and all together.

In a similar manner the Conjuror symbolises the intellectual faculties—age, science, righteous cant, solemnity, authority—which is why I make him so malicious.[99]

The action of this picaresque journey of autobiographical exploration and discovery takes place, for the most part, in three locations: ancient Greece, the Western Front, and London. Aldington's aim in embarking on this poetic journey "was to recapitulate his creative growth and personal disintegration."[100] In the extract given here, the narrator and Mezzetin, as privates, accompany the Conjuror, a Sergeant-Major, on a "stunt" across No Man's Land. The latter's stupid and thoughtless behavior betrays their position to the enemy, and Mezzetin is killed. This causes the narrator to wish for his own death as well, but, because of his self-confessed innate cowardice, he is unable to do so: "I wished a bomb would fall into my shell-hole, / For I felt too numb to stand up to the bullets."

A Dream in the Luxembourg takes up fifty-three pages (London: Heinemann, 1930). It is an erotic poem, dedicated to Brigit Patmore, whom Aldington first met in 1912. They had a brief liaison in 1912, a time when she was sexually attracted to H. D. as well as to Aldington. Then much later, in 1928, Aldington and Brigit Patmore embarked once more on a passionate affair that lasted until 1936.[101] The extract given occurs near the beginning, in section III. After the line, "Reported how many casualties?", an earlier version of the poem contained the following lines:

> It's a queer feeling that gets you at the heart,
> To walk back over the battle-ground
> And see the men you knew and liked
> Lying out there with the dew on their yellow faces,
> Odd battered figures in muddy khaki.
> And a queerer thing yet to see, as once I saw,
> A dead soldier still kneeling upright,
> Holding his rifle in his stiff clenched hand,
> With a long ghastly black-red stalactite of clotted blood
> Frozen from his mouth to his knee—
> An odd sight to come on in the pure November dawning.[102]

These lines do not appear in the first English edition. Aldington must have felt that the unmitigated presentation of this remembered sight would produce a feeling of unnecessary revulsion at this point in the poem, and that the less detailed and less insistent lines, "How many yellow dead men have I seen? / Carried how many stretchers? / Stood by how many graves—of young men too? / Reported how many casualties?", made his point with enough emphasis. The rejected lines are interesting, since they indicate to what extent Aldington, writing twelve years after the war, was still remembering its horrors in all their vivid intensity.

Life Quest is forty pages long (London: Chatto & Windus, 1935). It is the final poem by Aldington to contain a significant reference to the war. In his introductory note he advises the reader that it should not be taken as a narrative or philosophical poem, but as "a loose string of moods and meditations." In this extract the poet is taken unawares by a war memory. While walking by a river in France, his "blood hot with a long dream of love," the sight of a dead snake in the water connects immediately with the remembered sights of dead men. To reinforce the seamless sequence of images that begins at this point, Aldington abandons all punctuation in the section beginning, "I saw the white belly of the dead snake," and ending with, "With all the queer taut snake-life life gone limp and lost." The final image is a hallucination: he sees his own dead body floating, like the snake's, in the river. However, he is able to deal with this moment with equanimity. He reflects that his body, like the snake's and those of the war dead, will be reabsorbed into the natural world.

The Berkshire Kennet

[. . .]
O solitude, O innocent peace,
Silence, more precious than the Fleece
That Jason and his fellows sought,
Our greatest riches though unbought,
And hard to find and ill to praise
In noisy and mechanic days!
Yet in these humble meadows they
Have cleansed the wounds of war away,
And brought to my long troubled mind

161

The health that I despaired to find,
And, while their touch erased the pain,
Breathed the old raptures back again
And in their kindness gave to me
Almost that vanished purity.
Here where the osiers barely sigh
Hour upon hour still let me lie,
Where neither cannon roar nor noise
Of heavy wheels my ear annoys,
And there is none my face to scan
Save some incurious countryman;
[. . .]

1923

A Fool i' the Forest: A Phantasmagoria

[. . .]
So carry on, Sergeant-Major, carry on.

XXVI

I spoke the last words aloud
And they roused the Conjuror from sleep;
For it was night again.

He stood up and said:
'Get your rifles, men, and come along.'

Mechanically I arose and found my rifle,
Shook my pack and stood by Mezzetin,
Thinking: 'O my God, it's this misery again;
I've often thought I'd wake up from a dream
And find that we were back in it;
Well, it's no sillier than all the rest,
But the slavery of it's dreary.'

It appeared that Mezzetin and I were privates,
But the Conjuror (of course) was Sergeant-Major.
Off we went, to the music of night-firing,

The pleasant evening hymn of Lewis guns
And the pretty fire-works from the line.
The Conjuror led us down a sunken road,
Along the duck-boards of a trench—
As usual I caught my bayonet in wires,
Bashed my iron hat against a bridge
And wrenched my ankles on sixteen broken duck-boards.
At last we reached the front line;
A quiet relief—only two men hit.

The Conjuror bustled up and down,
Talking to officers and placing sentries;
Mezzetin and I hopped off,
Nipped into the signallers' dug-out,
And plotted how to steal the sergeants' rum.
But the Conjuror discovered us and said;
'I want you men to come with me;
I'm going on patrol.'
Mezzetin and I gazed wildly at each other;
I thought: 'Now I know this isn't true—
A Sergeant-Major on patrol!
It must be some dreadful nightmare.'
We went crawling out; the usual thing—
Shell-holes, puddles, sand-bags, knife-rests,
The regulation ration of skeletons, Mark VI.
All went well until we reached their wire;
I could see Mezzetin ahead of me
Caught on a rusty picket festooned with spikes,
Swearing in whispers like a perfect gentleman.
Then that damned Conjuror exclaimed:
'Look out! I see a Boche!'
Fired his revolver at a stump.
Of course I rolled into the nearest shell-hole;
Up went the Verey lights, down came minnies,
Rifle-bombs, grenades, rifle-fire,
And a beautiful scherzando of machine-guns.
Gradually the concert quieted down;
Suddenly I thought of Mezzetin
And knew he must be dead.
My heart went icy; I felt sick, sick,
And something vital left me for ever.

163

Then I knew that Mezzetin
Was as much to me as life itself;
I wished a bomb would fall into my shell-hole,
For I felt too numb to stand up to the bullets.

Who should remember you if we forget?
Those who lift top-hats and lay down wreaths?
Or those who buried you, dry-eyed and lousy?

The Conjuror crawled over to my shell-hole.
'Where's Mezzetin?'
'Why, dead, of course, what made you fire?'
'Where's his body?'
'Over by that picket, I suppose.'
He stood straight up; I whispered:
'Lie down, lie down, you'll draw their fire.'

Then I noticed a peculiar silence;
Not a gun, a shot, a light;
All was sinister and still.
I climbed from the shell-hole
And we walked towards Mezzetin.
There he lay, dead, dead, in mud and blood.
The Conjuror rolled him over, felt his heart:
'Yes, he's dead right enough.'
Then to my disgust and anguish,
He kicked the passive body, muttering:
'I'm glad he's dead;
I always hated and despised him,
With his eternal jangling mandoline
And stupid jokes at high and serious things;
Now he's gone, we'll make a man of you.'

I was aghast and trembling with rage.
Of course I know I should have killed him then,
But I always was a coward
And never could face the horror
Of jabbing a bayonet in a man's belly;
And as usual, my rifle was unloaded.
All I could do was gasp:
'You murderer, you murderer.'

XXVII

Here of course should come an elegy on Mezzetin;
But now he's dead I have no interest in writing.
Instead, I'll give you his obituary news.

On a wooden cross in France: 'R.I.P.
012342 Private Mezzetin. 1/7 Fool's Brigade.
Killed in Action. 1ˢᵗ April, 1917.'
In the 'List of Casualties':
The same, minus R.I.P.
In the 'List of Recent Wills':
'Sir Hanley Podge, broker, wholesale provision dealer,
Receiver of stolen goods, £1,325,498.
Mezzetin (the famous clown) £1.10 in silver.'
[. . .]

1925

A Dream in the Luxembourg

III

[. . .]
Yesterday I plucked out two grey hairs.
Memento mori. Yet a few more years,
And what remains of me and—hell!—of her?
Must fair women die?
I'll not believe it, Death is masculine.
Death, like a war-lord, wants more man-power,
And, by God, he gets it, I've seen him get it.

How many yellow dead men have I seen?
Carried how many stretchers?
Stood by how many graves—of young men, too?
Reported how many casualties?
But one gets used to it, quite used to it,

165

And it seems nothing for men to die,
Nothing for one to die oneself.
[. . .]

1930

Life Quest

Below the crooked bridge at Brantôme
The water of the Dronne runs clear and cold
Past the old garden of the monks.
I walked there in the bright September evening,
My blood hot with a long dream of love
And passionate yearning for life, more life.
The fire of my thought was hot and sweet,
Hiding with its gold haze the soft greensward
And the grey-brown trickling stream,
The last roses and the heavy elms.

With a swift shock my dream abandoned me
And the haze of fire was torn clear
For under an old willow I saw
The body of a dead snake in the water.
It was so dead, so utterly inert and dead,
Lying there, softly swaying in the water
On its back with its dead white belly
Turned under water to the sun
In a long slack curve pale and flaccid
Like a piece of old bleached rope
Swaying softly dead under the sun.

Now what I thought there I cannot tell you
For it was both more and less than thought—
I saw the white belly of the dead snake
And I saw the body of a dead English soldier
Laid like a coloured statue on the fire-step
I saw and the same sickly smell came choking
The body of a young German officer
His face blue-grey like his uniform

I saw the rag-clothed skeletons of Loos
I saw my own body lying white and helpless
Belly turned to the sun
Gently swaying in the water
Under the sunlight where the snake lay
With all the queer taut snake-life gone limp and lost.

I was not afraid, it was a great peace.

I saw that which was the snake
And myself and those others
Softly dissolve and drift with the stream
Down to the Dordogne
Down to the Gironde
Down to the great rollers of the sea,
And return as rain or cloud or air
But never again as a crisp-gliding snake
Rustling its way over dried grasses,
Never again as a human soul
Avid for much living . . .
[. . .]

1935

Select Bibliography

WORKS BY RICHARD ALDINGTON

All Men are Enemies. London: Chatto & Windus, 1933.

Collected Poems. New York: Covici, Friede, 1928.

The Complete Poems of Richard Aldington. London: Allan Wingate, 1948.

Death of a Hero. London: Chatto & Windus, 1929. (expurgated edition)

Death of a Hero. London: Consul Books, 1965. (unexpurgated edition)

A Dream in the Luxembourg Gardens. London: Chatto & Windus, 1930.

The Eaten Heart. London: Chatto & Windus, 1933.

Exile and Other Poems. London: George Allen & Unwin, 1923.

A Fool i' the Forest: A Phantasmagoria. London: George Allen & Unwin, 1924.

Images (1910–1915). London: The Poetry Bookshop, 1915.

Images. London: The Egoist Press, 1919.

Images of Desire. London: Elkin Mathews, 1919.

Images of War. London: C. W. Beaumont, 1919.

Images of War: A Book of Poems. London: George Allen & Unwin, 1919.

Images of War. Boston: The Four Seas Co., 1921.

Life for Life's Sake: A Book of Reminiscences. New York: The Viking Press, 1941.

Life Quest. London: Chatto & Windus, 1935.

The Love of Myrrhine and Konallis, and Other Prose Poems. Chicago: Covici, 1926.

The Poems of Richard Aldington. New York, Garden City: Doubleday, Doran, 1934.

Roads to Glory. London: Chatto & Windus, 1930.

Roads to Glory. London: Imperial War Museum, 1992.

War and Love (1915–1918). Boston: The Four Seas Co., 1919.

SECONDARY SOURCES

Barlow, Adrian. *Answers for my Murdered Self*. Francestown, New Hampshire: Typographeum, 1987.

———, ed. *Six Poets of the Great War*. Cambridge: Cambridge University Press, 1995.

Bergonzi, Bernard. *Heroes' Twilight: A Study of the Literature of the Great War*. London: Constable, 1965.

Blayac, A., and C. Zilboorg (eds.). *Richard Aldington: Essays in Honour of the Centenary of his Birth: Papers from the Montpellier Conference*. Montpellier, 1995.

Cadogan, Mary, and Patricia Craig. *Women and Children First: The Fiction of Two World Wars*. London: Victor Gollancz, 1978.

Cecil, Hugh. *The Flower of Battle: British Fiction Writers of the First World War*. London: Martin Secker & Warburg, 1995.

Coffman, Stanley K. *Imagism: A Chapter for the History of Modern Poetry*. Norman: University of Oklahoma Press, 1951.

Cole, Roger. *Gaudier-Brzeska: Artist and Myth*. Bristol: Sansom & Co., Redcliffe Press Ltd., 1995.

Crawford, Fred D. *British Poets of the Great War*. Selinsgrove: Susquehanna University Press, 1988.

Crawford, Fred D. *Richard Aldington and Lawrence of Arabia: A Cautionary Tale*. Carbondale: Southern Illinois University Press, 1998.

H. D. (Doolittle, Hilda). *Bid Me to Live (A Madrigal)*. New York: Grove Press, 1960.

Doyle, Charles. *Richard Aldington: A Biography*. London: Macmillan, 1989.

———, ed. *Richard Aldington: Reappraisals*. Victoria, B.C.: University of Victoria, B. C., 1990.

Dyer, Geoff. *The Missing of the Somme*. London: Hamish Hamilton, 1994; Penguin Books, 1995.

Ede, H. S. *Savage Messiah*. London: Heinemann, 1931. Bedford: The Gordon Fraser Gallery Ltd., 1971.

Friedman, Susan Stanford. *Penelope's Web: Gender, Modernity, H. D.'s Fiction*. Cambridge: Cambridge University Press, 1990.

Friedman, Susan Stanford, and Rachel Blau DuPlessis (eds.). *Signets: Reading H. D.* Madison, Wisconsin: The University of Wisconsin Press, 1990.

Gates, Norman T. *Richard Aldington: An Autobiography in Letters*. University Park, Pennsylvania: Pennsylvania State University Press, 1992.

———. *The Poetry of Richard Aldington: A Critical Evaluation and an Anthology of Uncollected Poems*. University Park, Pennsylvania and London: Pennsylvania State University Press, 1974.

Gindin, James. *British Fiction in the 1930s: The Dispiriting Decade*. London: Macmillan, 1992.

Gliddon, Gerald. *"When the Barrage Lifts": A Topographical History and Commentary on the Battle of the Somme 1916*. Norwich: Gliddon Books, 1987.

Guest, Barbara. *Herself Defined: The Poet H. D. and her World*. New York: Doubleday & Co., 1984.

Harmer, J. B. *Victory in Limbo: Imagism 1908–1917*. London: Martin Secker & Warburg, 1975.

Hughes, Glenn. *Imagism and the Imagists: A Study in Modern Poetry*. Stanford, Calif.: Stanford University Press, 1931.

169

Hynes, Samuel. *A War Imagined: The First World War and English Culture.* London: The Bodley Head Ltd., 1990.

Jones, Peter (ed.). *Imagist Poetry.* London: Penguin Books, 1972.

Kelly, Lionel (ed.). *Richard Aldington: Papers from the Reading Symposium.* Reading, 1987.

Kershaw, Alistair, and Frédéric-Jacques Temple (eds.). *Richard Aldington: An Intimate Portrait.* Carbondale and Edwardsville: Southern Illinois University Press, 1965.

Khan, Nosheen. *Not With Loud Grieving: Women's Verse of the Great War: An Anthology.* Lahore: Polymer Publications, 1994.

Klein, Holger (ed.). *The First World War in Fiction.* London: Macmillan, 1978.

McGreevy, Thomas. *Richard Aldington: An Englishman.* London: Chatto & Windus, 1931.

MacNiven, Ian S., and Harry T. Moore (eds.). *Literary Lifelines: The Richard Aldington-Lawrence Durrell Correspondence.* London: Faber & Faber, 1981.

Middlebrook, Martin. *The First Day on the Somme: 1 July 1916.* London: Allen Lane, 1971.

Monro, Harold. *Some Contemporary Poets.* London: Leonard Parsons, 1920.

Onions, John. *English Fiction and Drama of the Great War, 1918–39.* London: Macmillan, 1990.

Parfitt, George. *Fiction of the First World War: A Study.* London: Faber & Faber, 1988.

Parker, Peter. *The Old Lie: The Great War and the Public School Ethos.* London: Constable, 1987.

Pound, Ezra, *Gaudier-Brzeska: A Memoir.* Hessle, East Yorkshire: The Marvell Press, 1960. New York: New Directions Books, James Laughlin, 1960.

Pratt, William, and Robert Richardson (eds.). *Homage to Imagism.* New York: AMS Press, 1992.

Silber, Evelyn, and David Finn. *Gaudier-Brzeska.* London: Thames and Hudson, 1996.

Silkin, Jon. *Out of Battle: The Poetry of the Great War.* London: Routledge & Kegan Paul, 1972.

Smith, Richard E. *Richard Aldington.* Boston: Twayne Publishers, 1977.

Snow, C. P. *Richard Aldington: An Appreciation.* London: Heinemann, 1938.

Stead, C. K. *The New Poetic.* London: Hutchinson & Co., 1964.

Tate, Trudi. *Modernism, History and the First World War.* Manchester: Manchester University Press, 1998.

Taylor, Martin. *Lads: Love Poetry of the Trenches.* London: Constable, 1989.

Thorpe, Michael. *Siegfried Sassoon: A Critical Study.* Oxford: Oxford University Press, 1967.

Tylee, Claire. *The Great War and Women's Consciousness: Images of Militarism and Womanhood in Women's Writings, 1914–64.* London: Macmillan, 1990.

Wadsworth, Barbara, *Edward Wadsworth: A Painter's Life*. London: Michael Russell, 1989.

Zilboorg, Caroline. *Richard Aldington & H. D.: The Early Years in Letters*. Bloomington and Indianapolis: Indiana University Press, 1992.

Zilboorg, Caroline. *Richard Aldington & H. D.: The Later Years in Letters*. Manchester: Manchester University Press, 1996.

Index of First Lines